Security Operations Best Practices

Christopher J Brown

FireEye Press

FireEye Press Contact Information:
Email: press@fireeye.com

FireEye Contact Information:
Website: www.fireeye.com/company/contact-us.html
Technical Support: www.fireeye.com/support/contacts.html
Phone (U.S.): 1.877.FIREEYE (1.877.347.3393)

Contents

Introduction

About This Book

This book reflects the fusion between security operations, execution challenges and strategies as well as the more recent developments in the information security incident response and handling. Embracing change in a security operations environment that includes on-premise resources, cloud resources and a hybrid of both isn't easy. This book addresses many of the challenges that inhibit effective and outstanding security operations. It goes well beyond your typical "how to build a security operations center" guide to a broad body of knowledge, observations and information. The first chapters cover security operations from a strategic and foundational perspective. The later chapters address specific challenges and needs that are often overlooked when resources are limited, and can be read in any order.

Who Should Read This Book?

This book is intended primarily for information security but also for our peers and colleagues in the information technology business. Groups that can benefit include:

- Cyber security team leads
- Information security analysts, malware analysts, incident responders/handlers
- Security Operations Center Managers and Information Security Department Managers
- Chief information security officers and chief information officers
- Information security engineering teams
- Cyber security solutions architects of all types, from consumers/customers to vendors, developers and partners)
- Academic and university information security teams
- Information security professionals suffering from alert/event overload and general saturation
- Cyber security professionals interested in updating their skillsets to include virtualization and cloud security providers and platforms

About the Author

Christopher J Brown has over 35 Information Technology and Security certifications. He has spent 28 years in the Information Technology business, the last 15 of them dedicated to Information Security. He has taught at MIRCon and prior Cyber Defense Summits and delivered technical village talks at DEFCON. Mr. Brown has served as a consultant and defense contractor with multiple government security clearances, and held positions as a consultant and cyber security analyst at Northrop Grumman, Raytheon and DRS. He has also worked for ArcSight and as a Microsoft Trainer. He spent five years as a senior technical instructor for FireEye and delivers technical training domestically and internationally.

About the Technical Editors

Neil Lasher is a Technical Learning and Development professional with 40 years of IT experience. In his current role as Senior Technical Training Designer with FireEye Education Services, Neil has been instrumental in creating and delivering troubleshooting and forensic training materials for FireEye customers, partners, and Customer Support staff. Prior to FireEye, he served as Managing Partner at The Learning Coach, and CTO at Phone2Know.

Brian Shields is a senior cyber crimes analyst and security advisor. His efforts found advanced persistent intruders in the corporate network at Nortel. He has provided IT security support to the US government and designed custom detection mechanisms.

Ed Thornton is an Independent Computer Software Professional.

About FireEye Press

FireEye Press publishes real-world, field-tested best practices for FireEye network security technology, developed by FireEye support engineers and malware experts. FireEye Press books are available from most major online retailers.

Publisher and Editor: **Stella Hackell**
Designer: **Patrick Wilkes**
Executive Sponsor: **Michael Scruggs**
Email: **press@fireeye.com**

Acknowledgments

The first person I'd like to thank is my boss and by far, the best director I have worked for in the past 15 years, Vanessa Hanks. She is one of the most understanding, wise and accommodating bosses I have ever had the pleasure of working for. She also approved this book as a side project that I've been wanting to write for the past 2 years. I also thank my peers and colleagues at FireEye who have enriched my knowledge, are always "high speed and engaged" and have been a professional pleasure to work with over the past five years. A special thank you and acknowledgement to Stella Hackell, my main editor who kept me in line and on point, as well as the technical editors who contributed to the book, Neil Lasher, Brian Shields and Edward Thornton. I also thank Ruan Müller, for the input and context for the Security Orchestration chapter.

The team I worked with in Kuwait as a cyber security analyst and operations lead had a dramatic influence on my skills as an analyst and responder, including Jon Irizarry, Lyle Matsuoka, Gianni Vance, Steve Duong, Salah Sherriff, Travis Green, Chris White, George Tan and too many others to list. SANS Instructors that I have had the pleasure of learning from include Mike Poor, Ed Skoudis, John Strand and Ovie Carroll.   Phyllis and Clay Scott and Chuck Hernandez were my professional mentors.

Finally, I'd like to specifically acknowledge every student I have taught and every customer I have interacted with at FireEye, ArcSight, Microsoft, Hewlett Packard and in the US Army, Navy, Air Force and Marines. I learn new and exciting things from my students every day. It is an honor and a privilege.

Dedication

This book is dedicated to my family and one very special inspirational source. Although I've been professionally married to my employers over the years, my family has always loved and supported me. My dad, Robert Bernard Brown, always encouraged me to keep asking questions and technically growing, starting when I disassembled my first piece of electronics (and left the parts and pieces piled up on the floor). He told me, "Son, if you want to get out and experience the world, make sure you work in positions that require travel someone else pays for". That was some of the best advice he ever gave me, and I've been lucky and blessed to travel and teach both domestically and internationally. He has always been there for me.

My mom, Judith Ann Brown, who passed away in March of 2016 also encouraged and supported my technical growth. She saved until she could buy my first computer, a Commodore 64, when I was seven. I fell in love with computers then and still love them today.

My brother, Nicolas Noel Brown, has always been there and shares my quest to follow in the vocational and professional education footsteps of mom and dad. Nico – I love ya bro!

I originally got interested in information security when I read Clifford Stoll's "The Cuckoo's Egg". I will always consider Clifford Stoll my original inspiration to dedicate a career to information security. I was amazingly lucky to talk with him for a few hours a year ago. He embodies the original definition of the word hacker – one who strives to figure out and pursue the true meaning of everything possible. You have inspired, taught, mentored and delighted me over the years — thank you, Cliff!!

Chapter 1: SOS— Security Operations Scoping

Like many who enter technical careers, I was an amateur radio operator in my youth. At that time, knowledge of Morse code was a requirement for an operator's license. One of the most recognized phrases in Morse code is   ... ---... —the universal distress call, SOS. A popular (but incorrect) belief is that SOS stands for "Save Our Ship."

Here we're going to put out an SOS call—but for "Security Operations Scoping."

Scoping is where this book starts. You must know exactly what you are trying to detect, defend and protect. **You cannot secure what you are not aware of**. Some would say, "We want to protect everything". This quick answer is neither achievable nor possible.

Sadly, from my observation over the years in teaching hundreds of classes, most organizations do not scope enough. When a security organization is created, there are many discussions, plans, and scoping activities. However, over time, security operations scoping falls off and ceases to be a tactical, technical review of resources required to optimally perform the overall mission of security operations. Security operations scoping is only becoming more challenging when we consider the wider use of virtualization, cloud platforms and the dynamic nature of technology infrastructure changes. Less than a decade ago, most security teams did not actively manage cell phones—they were considered part of the telecom system, not mobile data devices. Given the rise in computing power of these devices, and the ubiquity of data in our pockets, it's hard to imagine not scoping them in today.

The variables to consider with mobile devices are in proportion to almost any other endpoint on your network. Scoping mobile devices to include iPhone and Android covers 99% of the current market. However, remember that other devices and operating systems are still in use, even if they are no longer sold. For example, should you scope Blackberry OS (Research In Motion) devices? Your organization may not support them--but hackers and threat actors aren't limited to the guardrails your organization has in place. You must decide whether your risk-based scoping plan allocates resources to such devices. Can you detect when a device running that operating system connects to your network?" A natural answer to that would be "That's not our job, that's network operations" or "That's an asset management problem". Hackers and threat actors thrive on the gaps inherent with complexity. Two of the biggest insider threat incidents of the past ten years went undetected because the threat actors—Edward Snowden and Chelsea Manning--knew exactly what was *not* being monitored.

So why doesn't scoping in security operations happen more often? Common reasons include the following:

- Scoping is seen as a one-time activity instead of an ongoing tactical assessment.
- Resources are not balanced between development operations (DEVOPS) and security operations (SECOPS) as the company grows.
- Resource constraints—lack of time, training, staff, or funding.
- Upper management does not fully understand the demands of security operations.

For example, after the Equifax breach in 2017, it came out that the chief security officer (CSO) had no background or experience in information security. In another example, one of the technical editors and endorsers of this book was on the Information Security team at Nortel. When he described news of an Adobe zero-day exploit during a conference call, a security operations executive responded, "Well, antivirus will protect us, right?" Zero-day exploits mean there is no product, sensor, or application that can detect the exploit. I don't fault anyone for not having a degree in the field, but there needs to be sufficient experience and knowledge.

Defining the Boundaries of Your Security Operations

The first step in scoping is to define the boundaries of your security operations scope. Boundaries are continually changing. Hackers, threat actors, even creative engineers and ingenious entrepreneurs strive to push boundaries to their limits and redefine traditional thinking. For some, fracturing or breaking boundaries is not enough; the goal is to demolish or eliminate them entirely. But you can't protect something you haven't defined.

Most organizations consider the scope of their security operations to be defined by the following:

- **Enclaves**—Sometimes associated with the term *perimeters,* enclaves are what is on the internal side of your firewalls. Cyber security incidents, compromises, intrusions and issues can be external to the enclave (perimeter) or internal.
- **Networks/Subnets** —Networks and subnets can be physical, based on buildings, locations, and segments, or can be logical, such as groups, organizations, and realms (in Microsoft Active Directory, *domains, forests* and *enterprises*).
- **Endpoints**—The devices on your networks. These typically include desktops, laptops, and servers. You may consider routers, switches, mobile devices, network attached storage resources, printers, point of sale terminals, and so on to be endpoints as well. Anything that has a hard drive or physical memory and network interfaces can be used maliciously.

Defining What You Protect

The subjects of defense and protection include multiple objects, groups, principals, and services. Remember from your information training the triad of "confidentiality, integrity and availability" (CIA). Here are just some of the things to consider:

- Operating systems
- Applications
- Public key infrastructure, cryptography, encryption
- Resources hosted in cloud platforms and through cloud providers
- Users of your network
- Endpoints
- Business partner access
- Third-party vendors
- Outsourcing. For example, do you run your own InfoTech/InfoSec ticketing system or is it outsourced to a contracted company? How do you validate confidentiality and integrity of your tickets when they are not under the control of your organization?
- Contractual rights regarding external parties. If you keep data in "the cloud" or you use outsourced systems, do you have the rights to conduct audits or do physical site/facility reviews? Does the external party's disaster recovery or business continuity planning provide the kind of coverage that the data requires?
- Mergers and acquisitions. Is there a plan for integrating acquired companies with your security operations?

Reviewing Your Detection, Defense and Protection Resources

Your detection, defense and protection resources should be reviewed regularly. Based on the size and scale of your organization, maybe it's once a year. If you're in a rapid growth trajectory or part of an organization that changes every few months, maybe it's quarterly.

Almost every organization has multiple detection, defense and protection resources, including but not limited to firewalls, intrusion detection and intrusion protection systems (IDS/IPS), anti-virus and anti-malware, data leak detectors, big data analytics resources, log aggregators, a Security Information and Event Manager (SIEM/SEM/ESM). Depending on the resource, especially when considering IDS/IPS or packet captures or web proxies, you might consider those more like detection grids or capture and collection nodes. Terms and scale vary, but you must have the right telemetry and measurement capabilities and processes in place.

Every detection, defense and protection resource, grid or node that you have has its own set of technical limits. Some adversaries, particularly the more advanced and organizationally funded groups, count on the technical limits of your detection, defense and protection resources as a part of their focused operations planning (we'll visit that topic in greater detail in Chapter 12). Some advanced threat actors have lab environments that strongly resemble a target organization's actual information security infrastructure. Their recon ranges widely, from scouring through your HR job descriptions or social media and technical blog or chat sites over a range of time to know exactly what products and platforms you have, to deploying malware into your environment designed to crawl and fingerprint the network and report back to "evil headquarters".

Larger organizations should have an information security engineering or support team that provides the right resources to answer questions such as:
- How many packets are dropped per sensor?
- What is the projected retention time for full packet captures across a specific segment of our network?
- At what point will our sensor or node drop into bypass mode or take itself offline?
- What protocols do we lack parsers for?

For medium-sized organizations that don't have an InfoSec Engineering group or dedicated full-time staff, hopefully someone in your information technology (IT) department specializes in the resources deployed for detection, capturing and evaluation of network traffic, packets or objects related to information security, protection, and so on.

Smaller organizations are the most resource constrained—your IT person or small team that is responsible for IT and information security (IS) may not have the resources to ask the right technical questions or to fully understand the answers. In this case, I recommend that you lean on your vendors or engage with consultants that can provide a technical scoping of the resources you have deployed.

In a mid-sized organization, although your reporting or departmental structure may not have changed for years, your network has changed. Your endpoints will change and evolve, your enclaves may change. It is extremely rare to find any organization that hasn't changed strategically, organizationally, or tactically and technically. There is always something that can be re-scoped.

Larger organizations have their own set of challenges to scoping. The larger an organization gets, the higher the probability that process and transparency will fracture (sometimes in multiple layers) to accommodate the needs of individual business units and their technological requirements. Larger organizations also are less agile when making changes – especially when there is a corporate-level or enterprise information security organization at the corporate level as well as subdivisions, business units or prior independent organizations that were part of a merger or acquisition. There is also a tendency in larger organizations to consider IT and IS operations long-term cost centers rather than profit centers.

Another challenge when you review your detection, defensive and protection resources is to consider whether your analysts, admins and engineers are properly trained to run specific products, platforms and resources. More than a few consultants and auditors have noted that administrative failings or lack of user training have caused resources to be underused or used ineffectively.

Continual Scoping

Part of security operations execution is continually assessing and evaluating your organization's ability to detect, defend and protect at multiple levels. As new threats emerge, and as threat actors continually evolve their exploits and droppers, part of scoping should be to evaluate and re-evaluate your capabilities.

It's not uncommon for mature, global, enterprise-level security operations organizations to have 30, 40, or more different applications, products, platforms, resources, and so on that vary across endpoints, network and enclave visibility. Some of those resources were "new technology" 15 - 20 years ago and could be far past their end of life (EOL). In a logging resource, something as minor as a field delimiter or character change can cause loss or deterioration of detection.

If a vendor updates a component, firmware, a signature or object-based engine, notifications can range from a major announcement to nothing more than a brief description in a field notice or readme file. It can't be stressed enough how important this is because we can't always count on errors or anomalies showing up when changes in detection mechanics work. One of the nasty little impacts in loss of detection is that you may **never** get feedback that detection capabilities have stopped. "The Sound of Silence" may be the only thing you'll notice when a detection capability fails. We call it "loss of EPS (events per second)." Review and rescoping are the best way to catch this kind of failure.

Understanding Where Your Data Is

In a commercial environment, an information security administrative team might have the following roles:

- **Security Administrator**—Responsible for tasks such as vulnerability scanning, operating system and application patching, endpoint baseline tracking, etc. Sometimes this position is referred to as the point person for "spraying scans and slinging patches". In the military, this position is called Information Assurance Security Officer (IASO).
- **Firewall and/or Proxy Administrator** —Responsible for firewalls, web proxies and enclave devices & network enclaves that operate as part of information assurance or cyber security. In the military, this position is called Information Assurance Network Manager (IANM).
- **Security Admin Team Lead**—Responsible for the implementation of policy at a technical level, interfaces with broader InfoSec or Information Technology structure and maintains status and operational supervisor tasks over the Security Administration team. In the military, this position is called Information Assurance Manager (IAM) and is also responsible for interfacing with US government or military leadership.

Some organizations combine those tasks and responsibilities with broader tasks under Information Technology job titles. However, one position that I have rarely seen is someone specifically tasked with understanding where the data in an organization is.

Many security organizations know where their physical assets are but they have no idea where their data is. Remember, **you CANNOT secure what you are not aware of**. You may not know where your data is, or you may have lost control of your data. If you or your team hands your data over to a cloud provider, it's easy to lose track of it. Some industries or countries, especially those covered under regulations or compliance (such as HIPAA in the US or GDPR in Europe), are required to know what and where their data is. Scope or discovery of this type becomes becomes challenging the more your organization changes. The days of having all your data reside in data centers that you control are coming to an end.

Today, your data will be in one or more of the following locations:

- **Physically onsite**—Data hosted on your physical site—for instance, in servers or storage devices in your server room or data center.
- **Physically offsite**—Data stored on individual backup drives, USB drives, or even on mobile devices. These are typically under the control of the employee and not the IT or IS department.
- **Hybrid and cloud**—Some data is hosted physically onsite and some is hosted through a cloud provider. For example, the back-end email servers that are physically deployed in

your data centers may use Unix-based Sendmail or Postfix, while the front-end email servers are hosted through Office 365 or Gmail.

- **Cloud hosted**—100% of specific types of data are hosted at a cloud provider or multiple providers, not within the physical control of your organization.

When data is stored in a cloud or hybrid system, the complexity of keeping track goes up. It is relatively easy to go find SERVER-001 in Building 3, Rack 4. It's not so easy to find "virtual container 3" or "virtual bucket A" in cloud platform "X".

Your data is critical. Without it, your business would grind to a halt. The touch points for your data are equally critical. Was a recent exploit publicly disclosed that impacts a widget used by your cloud provider? You may never know until an incident, data breach, data leak, compromise or intrusion is detected. Was a recently disclosed vulnerability found in an enterprise database product your company depends on to host critical customer records?

Five years ago, a cloud provider used a processor chip on hardware running virtual servers that was determined to have a flaw in Ring0 processing that could allow users in virtual environments to escalate user-level privileges to admin privileges. If you wanted to validate that your cloud provider isn't vulnerable to that hardware flaw, can you even ask that question as part of the agreement you signed with your cloud provider?

Pervasive Visibility

A new security organization might start out strong with this concept. However, as complexity creeps in or as decisions are made to cut costs, transparency or visibility within your own organization can quickly be lost. There is an old saying in the technical field service industry, "You can pay me now or you can pay me later but eventually, you're going to pay". There is a parallel phrase to that in cyber security, "You can secure this now or you can secure it later, but one way or another, this needs to be secured". Experience has taught me not to wait until later to secure something that has recently changed.

This isn't news to anyone working the front lines of information or cyber security. When you engage in scoping, a key question to ask is: Where have we lost visibility recently? You might be surprised at the answers you hear. A shift in technology could render an entire team blind to segments of data that they need to do their jobs.

Loss of visibility can happen when a major application is migrated into the cloud, such as access logs in a database. It may have been easy to collect or capture logs when the database was hosted on a SQL server sitting in your data center. Once that server is migrated into the cloud, some cloud providers will charge for how much data you pull through their cloud. When a decision is made to "optimize" or "cost reduce" in one area, costs in another area can increase in proportion.

It is not wise to assume your cloud provider is responsible for any aspect of cyber security relating to your organization. Most cloud providers have clear definitions of what they will be responsible for, what YOU are responsible for and what would be considered shared responsibilities. It's also dangerous to assume that the method with which you've collected or captured logs on a physically local resource will work the same way with a cloud-hosted resource. Yet many organizations make those assumptions without reading the fine print.

Here's an example of a pervasive visibility blocker. Many years ago, I often needed to fingerprint a system or get more details about a host on the network. The quickest way to do that was to fire up a session with something we called a "jump box" that was a on a detection grid that we controlled. We'd swing over to the jump box to access an intrusion detection sensor closest to where we thought a host might be. From there, we would attempt to run something as simple as a netstat or use WMIC (Windows Management Instrumentation Console) to log in remotely to a system and run the equivalent of a system info command. Easy enough—except when we were blocked by a firewall or internal proxy. Adjusting the firewall or proxy to pass commands from the jump box or remote system wasn't covered under our contract; it was covered by a different contractor. That would be considered a PVB or a "pervasive visibility blocker". This kind of challenge or blocker is NOT what you want to run up against when you're in the middle of analyzing or working an incident.

Other issues, such as updating from SSL to TLS, can break monitoring techniques.

When it comes to cloud providers, even if you think you don't need it now, you should have a "go to" resource on the security team who deals with all of the cloud providers you interact with. The wrong time to realize you need access to those points of contact is in the fog of an incident. Especially when everything is blowing up and you are receiving rapid-fire fragments of information that may or may not be directly related to what you're working on.

Chief Information Security Officer

Knowing where the data is, maintaining pervasive visibility, and scoping and rescoping your security operations often fall to a chief information security officer (CISO) or their deputy. A CISO typically reports to the chief information officer (CIO). The CIO's number 1 job is to ensure that computer and network operations work 24x7, 365 days a year. Unfortunately, information security is often perceived as "getting in the way of operational requirements". The CISO's observations, assessments and recommendations may be overridden or downplayed as not important to the CIO's primary task/responsibility. When there is a potential conflict of interest in reporting to the CIO, consider moving the CISO to report directly to the CEO or another C-level position, such as the chief operations officer or the chief technology officer. From an operational perspective, keeping endpoints, servers, networks and systems up and running will always have a priority over everything, but you can reduce conflicts of interests in reporting structure.

Soft Spots and Gray Zones in Your Operations

A security organization will always have some weak areas of infrastructure, the network, specific hosts or groups of hosts or maybe even within your own detection and protection capabilities. They change from time to time. While it would be extremely valuable to have a heat map that can quickly display where those soft spots are, they are not that easy to keep track of.

My first time driving on a German autobahn was quite the experience because growing up in the United States, I had always heard, "You'll love driving in Germany on the autobahn. There are no speed limits!" When I saw a white sign with "160" or "140" in a red circle, I assumed it was simply a recommendation. It wasn't until I fractured a few German speeding laws and paid a few fines that I asked the Polizei what the real story is about the autobahn being "speed free". Their answer was that most of the Autobahn was speed free, but speed limits were posted around exits and in areas where accidents were common.

The German police had identified danger spots on the autobahns and added extra protection in the form of speed limits. A strategy for identifying areas of your security operations where you need extra detection and defense is to look at where you have had incidents, intrusions, breaches or compromises in the past. (Another strategy is to integrate cyber threat and intelligence resources with your daily security operations, as we discuss in Chapter 11.)

Gray zones are areas of over-detection in your networking infrastructure. Gray zones produce many events or alerts that did not originate in real security incidents. A common cause of gray zones is the strategy of deploying your entire IDS signature set across every sensor and every segment of your network, regardless of the context or the resources in each area. Our cyber security analytic group was once flooded with multiple Snort/IDS alerts about abnormally large packets in a certain area of the network, which appeared to indicate a data leak incident or exfiltration event. A few hours into the investigation, a local system admin said, "I wonder if this is because of the VMware servers we just stood up a few days ago?" VMware has a feature called dynamic resource allocation (DRA). If a virtual host runs short of a resource like memory or hard disk space, DRA identifies under-utilized and over-resourced virtual components and dynamically allocates their resources to the virtual host in need. The Snort/IDS signature that was firing excessively was doing its job by alerting us to activity that it did not understand but that was benign.

If we had pervasive visibility, we could have tuned or removed the IDS signature from the sensor closest to the segment servicing VMware stacks and prevented the fire drill. This gray zone is an example of something worth knowing about, but not a true positive our team would consider a security event or incident.

Enhanced Scoping Based on Geopolitical Risk

If your organization operates sites in countries with elevated geopolitical risk, your security operations scoping might need to include extra integration with physical security. Setting up shop without extra security in countries known for engaging in cyber economic espionage is like leaving the doors unlocked and windows open. For example, China has a reputation for engaging in cyber economic espionage that cross the traditional boundary of nation-state to nation-state espionage. If your company decides to do business in China, it cannot rely on the same risk profile and detection methods you would consider in countries like the US, Canada, or Australia. Doing so could be considered negligence and dereliction of duty.

Brian Shields, one of the technical editors and endorsers of this book, recalled a US company that had an international business office in France in which high-level sales discussions took place. The office noticed a sudden loss of sales that persisted over several quarters. A team of counter-intelligence experts performed a sweep of the building and discovered listening devices in the conference room.

In January 2002, China claimed to have found over 30 surveillance bugs, including one in the headboard of the presidential bed, aboard a Boeing 767 that was recently purchased from Delta Airlines. I can't speculate about whether the claim was valid or whether the airline was aware, but there are certainly organizations, both US and foreign, that would have an interest in planting surveillance devices near foreign leaders.

Pitfalls of Scoping

Although rarely a problem, hyperactive scoping or scoping too frequently can be equally bad. You don't want to scope so often that you're always redefining operations or adjusting fire so quickly that the rest of your organization or security team can't keep up.

Another pitfall is scope creep. When you're new to an organization and want to make a name for yourself, it's easy to rush into decisions or attempt to include areas in security operations that may be covered by another team or that you're not resourced to handle. Scope creep can also hurt if you quickly make too many conclusions or start writing checks that your team cannot cash.

More than a few team leads, supervisors, managers, etc. have asked me "What would you do if you were new to an information security group, but you really had an idea that you thought could impact an organization?". That kind of question both intrigues and infuriates me. The intriguing part is that I want to answer and show that I can implement new strategy or tactics that can make a positive impact to the department, for my boss, and for the company. The infuriating part is that sometimes questions are asked but not for the reason we think. It can be fun (but precarious) to turn that question around and ask, "What has worked in the past when others have had good ideas but were new to the organization?"

As much as you think an idea might be new or innovative, chances are, especially with more mature, established information security organizations, that your idea has been discussed in the past. One example, and it comes up a lot these days, is going from HTTP to HTTPS. While it's technically possible to do all kinds of things with HTTPS—dissect it at the firewall, deploy SSL interception products or platforms, maybe have your proxies pick apart SSL—the infrastructure might not be able to support everything. Likewise if your detection, defensive and protection resources are integrated with SSL interception products that work with SSLv2 and not SSLv3The organization may have a very good reason for their decisions.

Having an open mind when you're scoping is important and soliciting technical and management observations from your peers is essential before presenting new ideas into your security operations. As for the original question, a safe answer would be along the lines of "I'd like to listen to the context and history that my colleagues can offer and consider the positive and negatives of proposing new ideas or increasing/changing the scope of how we handle security issues".

Many of the issues that we face today in security operations have no yes or no, right or wrong answer. It's all about shades or layers of positives and negatives, advantages and disadvantages. The level of support you get when you collectively bring up new ideas or change the scope of anything is directly related to how much you've learned before you make a suggestion or submit a proposal.

Scoping can hurt if you rush into changes too soon and don't consider the feedback or observations of the team that will be impacted by the changes. Projects take time to develop and rushing to a conclusion that something works or hasn't worked can be as bad as taking too long to make the same conclusion. Scoping too often can be frustrating and generate all kinds of problems.

99% market share for iOS and Android: https://www.statista.com/statistics/266572/market-share-held-by-smartphone-platforms-in-the-united-states/

Equifax breach: https://www.nbcnews.com/business/consumer/equifax-executives-step-down-scrutiny-intensifies-credit-bureaus-n801706

Claims of bugs aboard a 767:

https://www.telegraph.co.uk/news/worldnews/northamerica/usa/1382116/China-finds-spy-bugs-in-Jiangs-Boeing-jet.html

Chapter 2: Knowing What's Normal

The problem statement for this chapter is, "How can you detect abnormal or malicious activity if you don't have a solid reference for what is normal and benign?" You need to know what normal traffic looks like on your network in order to recognize abnormal behavior effectively. There never seems to be enough time to get to know the baseline, so many organizations rely on their information security infrastructure to detect intrusions and threats. But malicious behavior does not always generate alerts. You need a plan for detecting malware when you have almost nothing to go on—not just once, but several times per year, because normal behavior may change as your network conditions change over time.

Many good security operations specialists, cyber security analysts and InfoSec warriors use gut feelings or intuition based on years of experience. I firmly believe that intuition is important, but it's equally important to identify normal conditions concretely. Knowing what patterns are normal is like setting up a control against which you can compare a variable. I always hated setting up a control in chemistry class, because I wanted to get right into the fun of combining chemicals to see what would happen. Over the years, though, I have come to realize that the topic I hated is an important requirement and something that is easy to take for granted.

Without a control and a variable, there is no way to compare states or conditions. Without a control and a variable, measurement becomes very difficult and sways from quantitative to qualitative and subjective. In security operations, unless you put the effort in to collect, capture, and define a control in the form of normal and benign behavior, and later compare that to a variable, it will be very hard to recognize abnormal or malicious behavior.

Here is an example. I was on a hunting mission, examining packet captures to see what was out there, when I stumbled across strings like the following:

```
/0576547258799103485b/send  or  /124879531564797979799/stop
```

Random strings of numbers following the same format, with end statements like *send, stop,* and *continue* looks like command and control traffic from malware. But if it was command and control traffic, why was there so much of it in our packet captures? After looking at the source and destination IP addresses, it didn't take long to figure out that although these were command and control packets, they weren't malicious. That's what YouTube traffic looked like back in 2012 and 2013. (Since then, YouTube has switched from HTTP to HTTPS, which means the packet payload is encrypted.) A lot of users on the network happened to be watching YouTube videos when I went on that brief threat-hunting mission.

Challenges to Knowing Normal

Depending on the size and layout of your organization, reasonable questions like, "How many company-authorized applications are included in our baselines?" or "How many baselines do we have?" can be challenging and extremely time consuming to answer. You need to know what company-authorized applications users have in your baseline as well as staying up to date on threats, exploits and vulnerabilities. For many organizations, baselines, applications supported, configuration and change management are not even in the wheelhouse of an information security group—they are part of Information Technology.

From a security standpoint, the word *baseline* refers to the operating system and application loads or image your company or organization supports on endpoints. Those endpoints can include laptops, desktops, tablets, field devices, servers, virtual hosts, cloud-hosted resources, and so on. However, there are many other aspects beyond endpoints:

- The hardware configuration of your various hardware platforms, servers, desktops, laptops, and so on.
- The configuration of your network infrastructure devices such as switches, routers, aggregators, proxies, firewalls, load balancers and scaling devices, and so on.
- Network segment baselines – how much traffic is "normal" or "average" for segments of your network. This can be measured by trending based on bandwidth utilization, flow statistics, protocol telemetry.
- Operating system components for various versions of Microsoft Windows, Apple macOS, Google Android, and flavors of Linux or Unix. Not just the components themselves but also how they boot, how they shut down, what makes them tick.
- Browsers, plug ins, add-ons and normal functionality within the various browsers that are deployed throughout your enterprise.
- Applications.
- Virtual machine infrastructure, including your cloud providers.
- Business partner connections and remote access points.
- Internet access points are (easy to track in a small network; not so easy as organizations grow).
- All the DMZs and all the VLANS throughout your enterprise.
- Enterprise-level services such as DNS, LDAP and Active Directory, which also need their own baselines.

"Normal" may also include unwanted network traffic resulting from misconfigurations, defective equipment, bots, scripts, scans and so on. Capturing a certain level of noise will be inevitable. For instance, if you log "access denied" events on enclave firewalls, there will be so many that it's easy to get lost. When enclave firewalls are near servers or appliances, it's advisable that someone review your denied logs.

©FireEye 2019

A good place to start is to figure out how you're going to capture, collect or define your normal so you have a control to reference.

Tools for Capturing the Control

The decision to have a reference or a control already puts you ahead. Most information security specialists are thrown into the fire of tens of thousands of events and alerts to triage, not enough time to work on everything, and no reference point for typical endpoint traffic. By asking around, you might even be able to get a detailed document on what an average endpoint baseline is. When I taught Information Assurance for the US Army in Europe as a contract trainer in 2004, we had a guide titled something like "Windows XP: Applying a Security Baseline," and it was more than 80 pages. It wasn't long before the chain of command realized that engaging with an 80-page document for every single desktop or laptop was too time consuming. To do quick and effective baselining and system imaging, the Department of Defense Information Systems Agency (DISA) developed the "Army Gold Disc" and "DISA Gold Image". Unfortunately, there were soon so many baselines that I had to ask, "Whose baseline are you using?"

When you ask what your company or organization uses for an endpoint baseline, don't be surprised if the answer is something like, "We have an image that gets pushed out via a standard endpoint security agent."

To develop a control, we need to go deeper than image deployment into what the baseline includes and how it's measured. Knowing you have a Ford, Chevrolet, Audi, BMW or Mercedes car means you know who manufactured the vehicle. It doesn't tell you how the engine performs under various loads and in various gears, what type of electrical system it has, or how the brake system was designed.

You wouldn't consider driving a vehicle without a fuel gauge, a speedometer, or temperature gauges. Yet many organizations are doing just that by lacking the proper recording, measurement, snapshotting or telemetry of their baselines or control to compare with a variable.

Before you start, determine how deep you can go. Here are some levels that apply to gathering a baseline:

- Host Profiling:
  - Operating system standard build received by the endpoint manufacturer/vendor
  - Operating system "customized" build ready to roll into production
  - Operating system after you've applied your baseline or endpoint image

- Network Profiling:
  - o Port and protocol activity
  - o The services typically run over various segments/enclaves/subnets of your network
- User Profiling (remember that users are constantly changing):
  - o What users typically log in to specific endpoints
  - o What activity is typically expected for certain types of users (per department, per job function, per task or mission)
  - o Specific activities conducted by built-in accounts such as Administrator or Guest accounts on Windows and Root or SUDO accounts on Linux. (Most built-in, local, higher-privilege accounts should not be included. Use of these accounts may indicate malicious intent or at the very least an abnormal use case.)

Now let's go into some of the resources you can use to gather measurements and telemetry within a Microsoft Windows environment.

OS and Application Tools

Microsoft Baseline Security Analyzer (MBSA) (Figure 1): https://www.microsoft.com/en-sa/download/details.aspx?id=7558
MBSA was introduced by Microsoft in 2004. Although it hasn't been updated since 2015, it is still useful but it has its caveats as well. MBSA helps you determine how secure the configuration of a Microsoft operating system is.

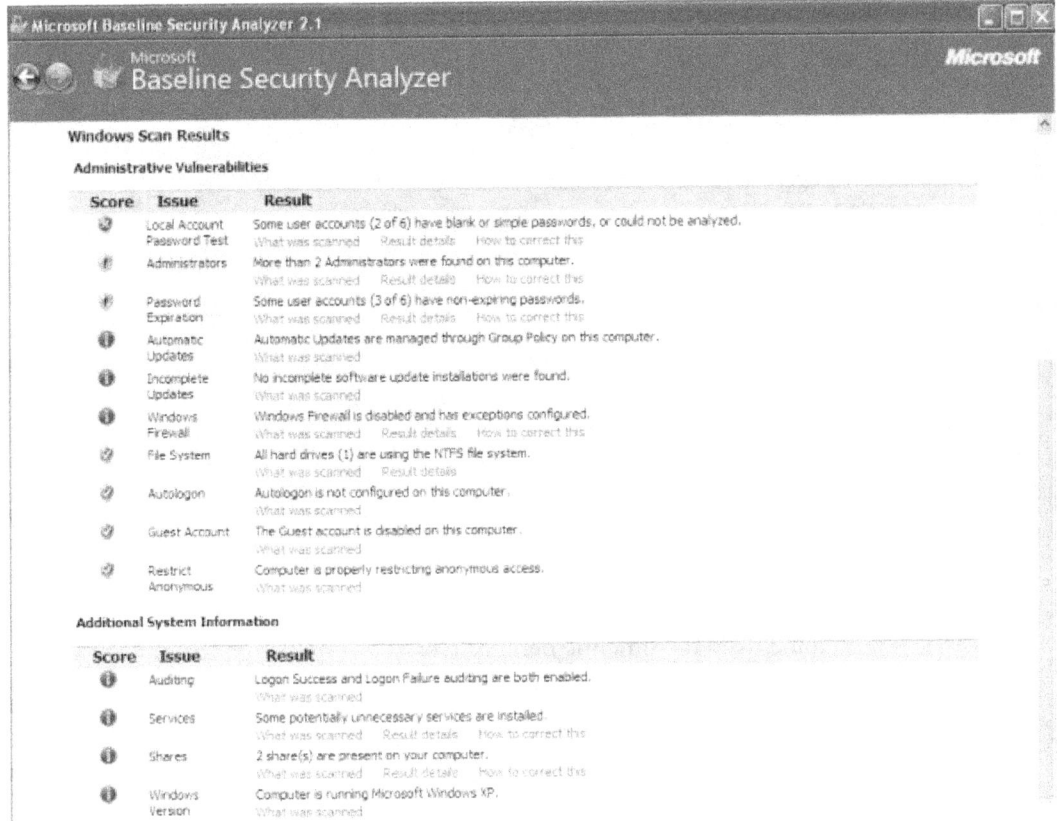

Figure 1: Microsoft Baseline Security Analyzer

For this type of control, we also need to get a handle on what a typical file and folder structure looks like, which processes and services are present and running, what the registry looks like, and so on.

Redline (Figure 2): https://www.fireeye.com/services/freeware/redline.html
Redline is freeware that originated from Mandiant. Redline is a great way to run a standard or comprehensive collector all the way up to capturing memory images for use with complementary memory analysis resources.

Figure 2: Redline

Figure 3 shows a view of Redline from the timeline perspective:

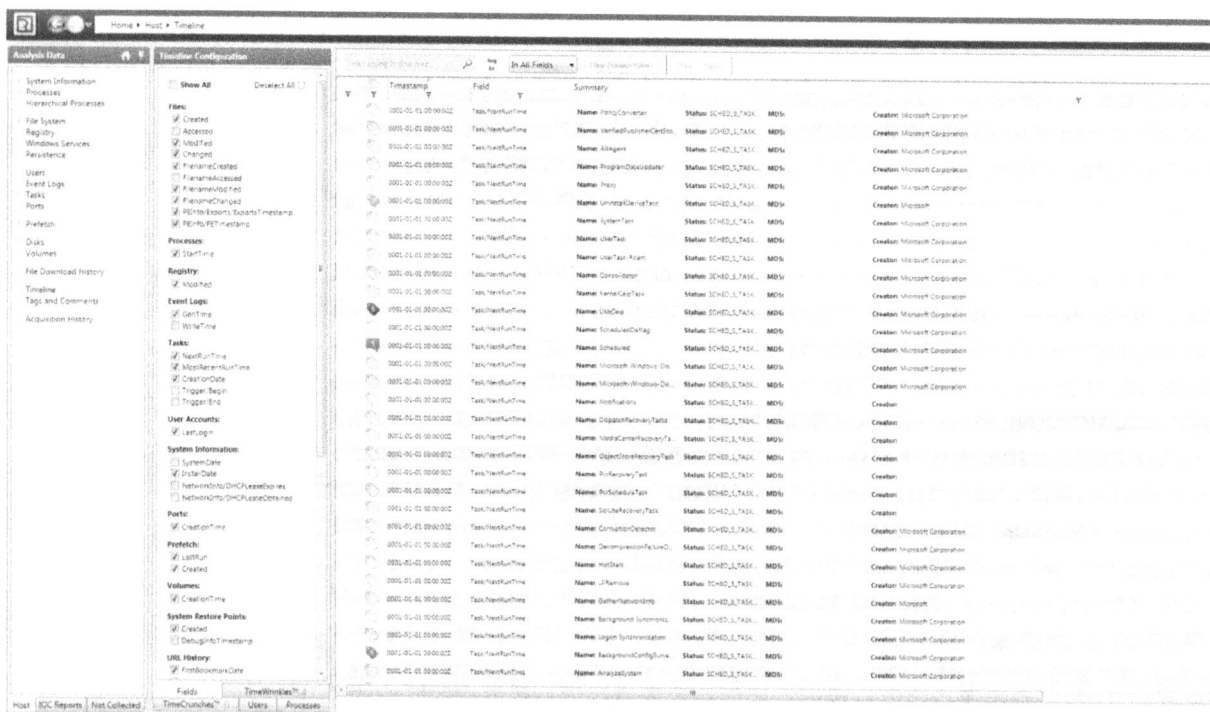

Figure 3: Timeline view in Redline

Many resources are available for Redline training, including the documentation, YouTube videos, and professional-level, commercially available training that includes Redline in the course curriculum.

There are a few things to remember when using resources like Redline or MBSA:

- The *wrong* time to collect or capture data regarding your control is during or after an incident. When an incident has happened, you are now working with the variable. We'll cover that in the next section.
- You don't know what you don't know. If you have been hacked but the hack or intrusion has not been detected, the data you capture will be contaminated. If your virtual private networks (VPNs) or the remote desktop protocol (RDP) are being used maliciously, your control will be contaminated.
- It's easy to gather information on an individual system. Scaling across multiple endpoints is more challenging

Both Redline and Microsoft Baseline Security Analyzer focus on the operating system level, providing less information about states of things like applications or the registry. Although both Redline and MBSA can collect and capture information regarding applications and the registry, neither can take snapshots for comparison of before and after.

Registry Snapshots and Installation Monitors

Regshot (Figure 4): https://sourceforge.net/projects/regshot/
Regshot is a good tool for registry snapshots:

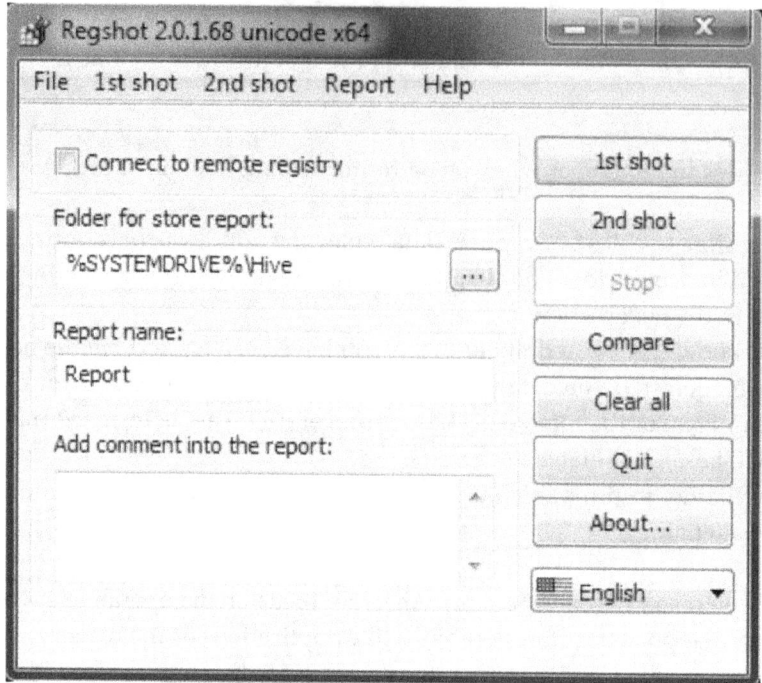

Figure 4: Regshot

Installation Managers or Monitors typically don't provide functionality for comparing before and after, but they can record what has changed as applications (or malware) are installed and deployed locally on an endpoint. For practical purposes, I like to consider these like the big brother or sister to the Unix *tail* command. A few examples of these:

SysAnalyzer (Figure 5): http://sandsprite.com/blogs/index.php?uid=7&pid=185

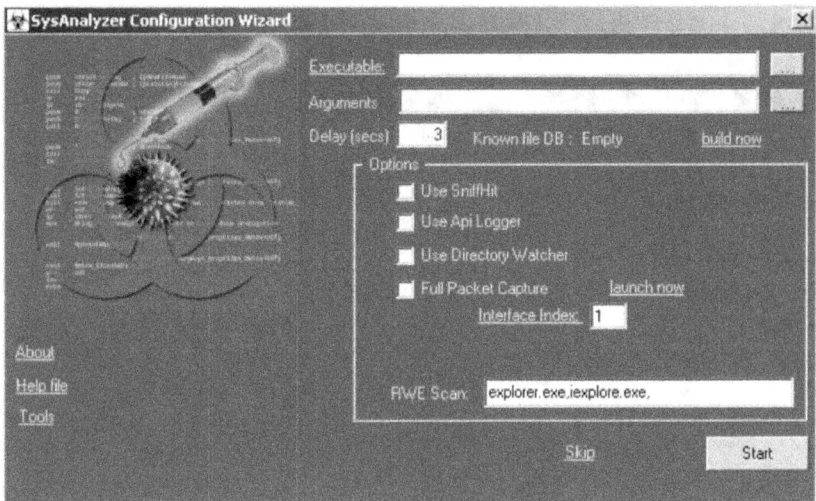

Figure 5: SysAnalyzer

Here is an example of the SysAnalyzer API Logger (Figure 6):

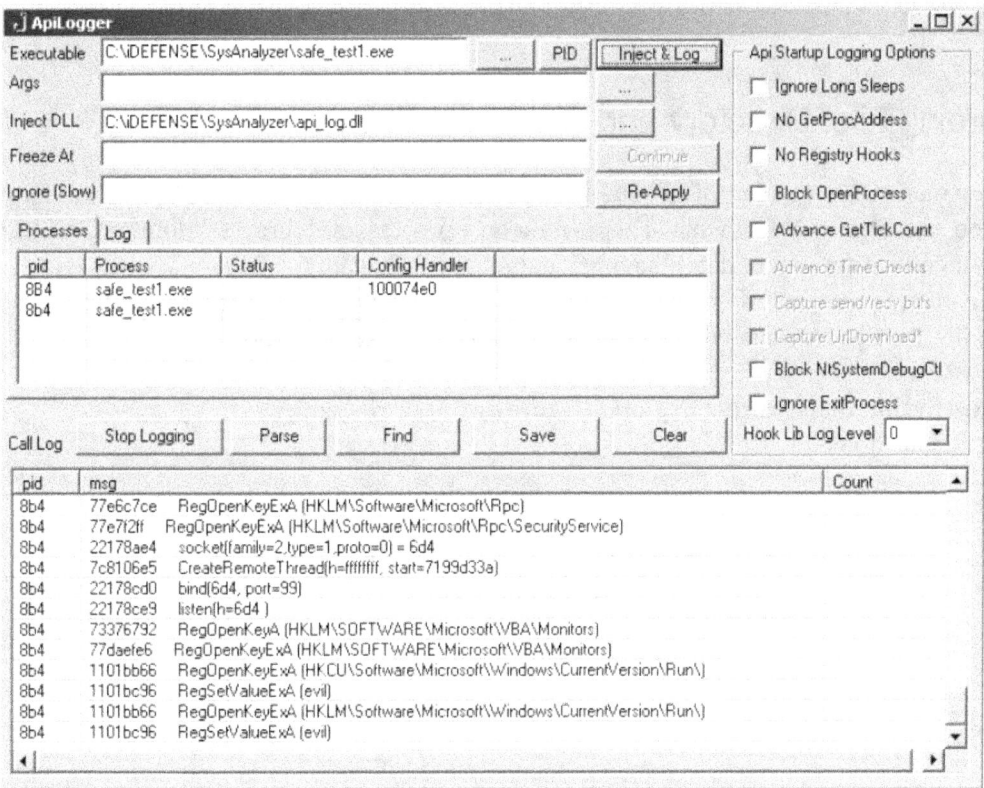

Figure 6: SysAnalyzer API Logger

InstallSpy (Figure 7): http://www.2brightsparks.com/assets/software/InstallSpy_Setup.zip

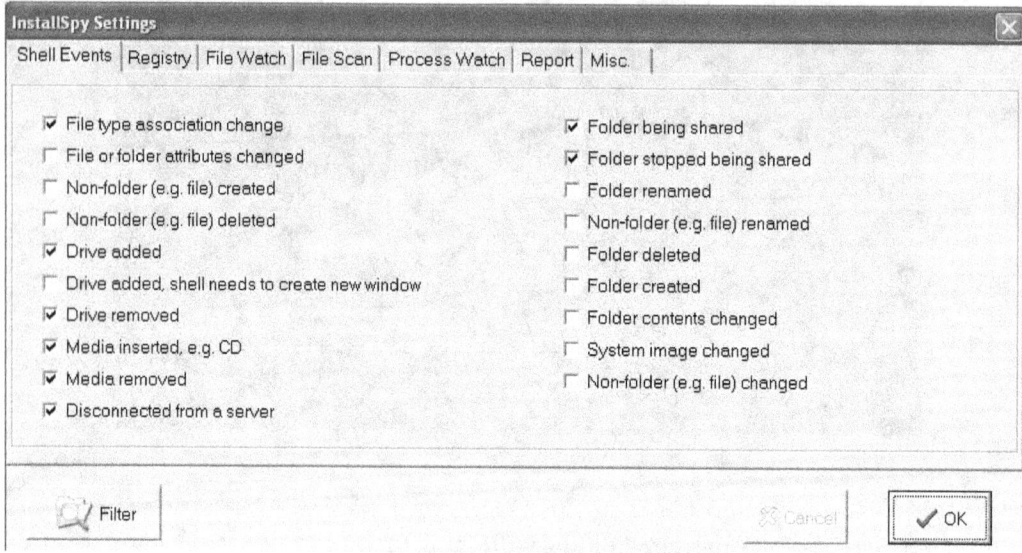

Figure 7: InstallSpy

Recording File, Directory and Process Activity

There are many resources for this. I usually recommend Windows Sysinternals. Process Explorer gives you a real-time view of what is happening on a process level. Process Monitor can filter and log a tremendous amount of data—so much data that you'll want to get very familiar with pivoting, filtering, tuning and pruning, slicing and dicing through what can be captured. Without those skills, the flood of data will be difficult to manage and understand.

Windows Sysinternals Process Explorer (Figure 8): https://docs.microsoft.com/en-us/sysinternals/downloads/process-explorer

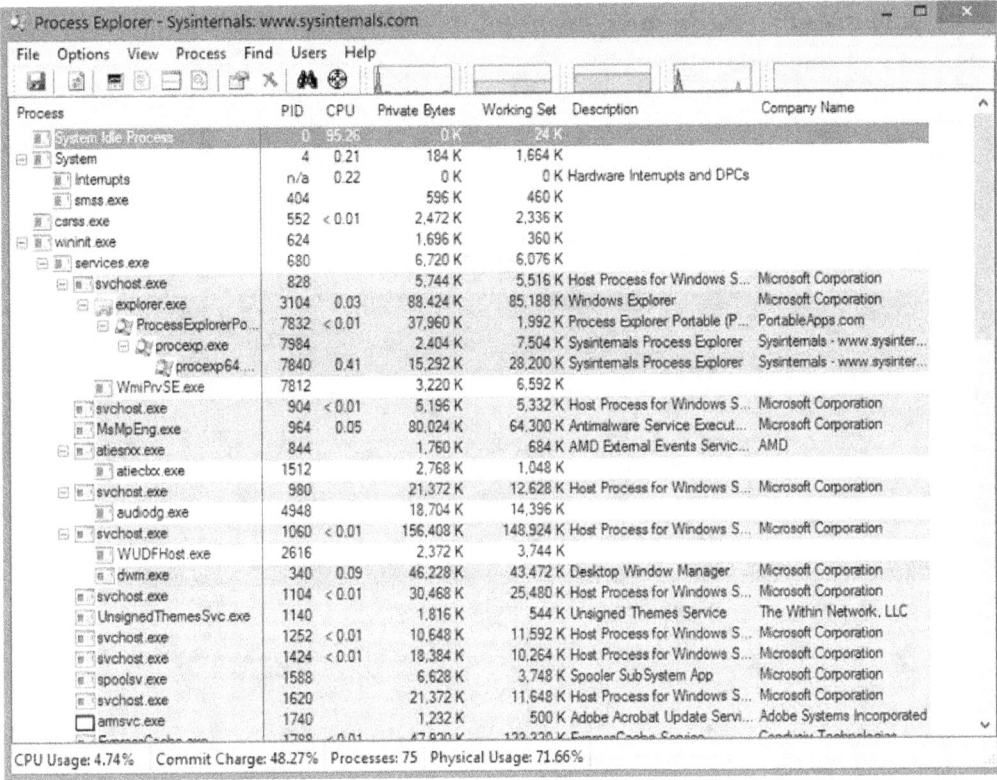

Figure 8: Process Explorer

Windows Sysinternals Process Monitor (Figure 9): https://docs.microsoft.com/en-us/sysinternals/downloads/procmon

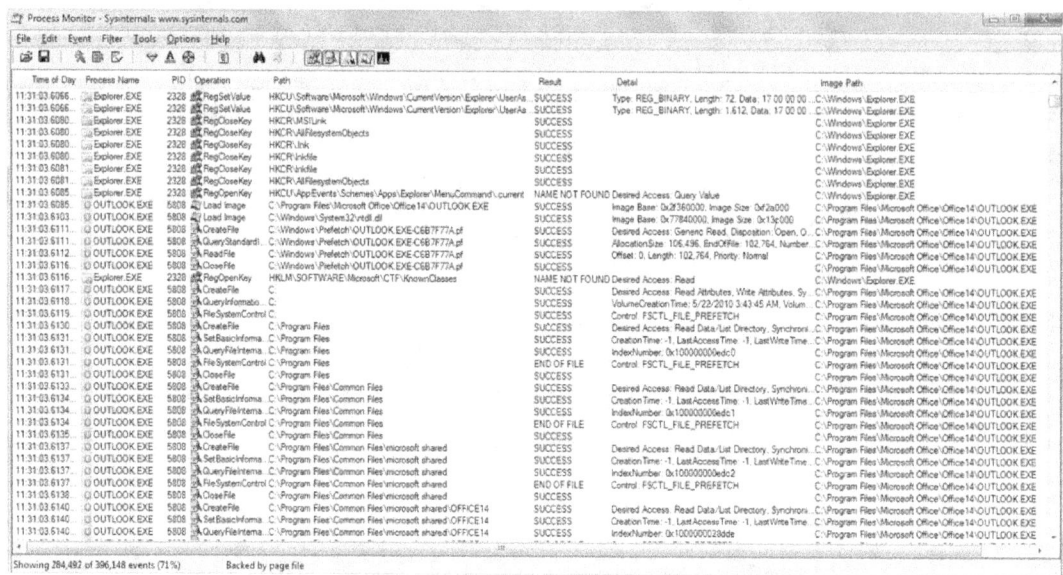

Figure 9: Process Monitor

Regarding network activity, a sniffer such as WireShark or TShark can help. So can Netresec Network Miner or Nirsoft SmartSniff.

API Monitors and Managers

One of the best ways to capture details about your endpoint's applications and how they interact with the operating system is to monitor API (application programming interface) activity.

API Monitor (Figure 10): http://www.rohitab.com/apimonitor

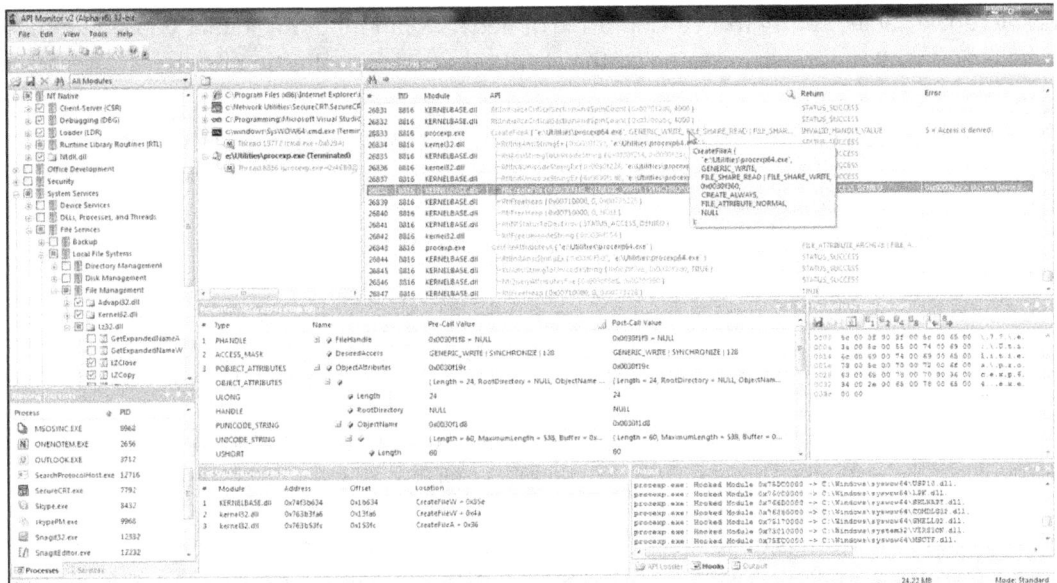

Figure 10: API Monitor

Warning: Ensure you are downloading these resources from a safe and reputable source! The best source is the author or publisher of the application. We've made a best effort at ensuring the links above are open source, from their original author or publisher, and clean and free from any malfeasance. Other sites host what appear to be the same applications. Tread cautiously when downloading from such sources—they may be clean or so corrupted that you need a tetanus shot after visiting them.

If you use safe tools or resources on a system that has a rootkit, you can no longer trust the results of anything. Once you suspect integrity has been lost, you can no longer completely trust anything running on the host. This is why forensics analysts typically boot from sources other than the disk or volumes they are trying to analyze.

Tools for Capturing the Variable

Once you have defined your endpoint control, it's time to have a variable for comparison. Sometimes this is referred to as "delta analysis" or determining what has changed from the control to the variable. The activities to capture and collect content to a variable are the same as those to capture and collect data associated with your control. You'll do the same things after malware is installed, deployed or provisioned within the endpoint. That isn't an easy process. The resources referenced in the previous section (except Regshot) were not designed to compare two data sets.

It's best to do variable capture from a USB drive or network mount point so that you don't foul your collection with the activity created by the act of capturing or collecting itself.

Multiple monitors and plenty of RAM will be your friend. Attempting to do this on a 12" or even a 15" laptop screen is painful. For instance, Redline is awesome at showing the results of a single system. If you want to compare system A to system B, you need to bring up 2 instances of Redline. Be careful with this; you'll quickly start chewing through RAM when you bring up more instances of Redline on the same host.

FireEye Network, Email, File Security and AX Platforms

Continual work is required to pick apart baselines, determine controls, run variables, measure the deltas between the two, determine levels of maliciousness, and so on.

Much of the variable work is done for you by the FireEye Network, Email and File Security Platforms (NX, EX, and FX Series) and the AX Series platform. The OS Change Detail Report tracks objects or malware, chronologically, as they are run and detonated in the protected environments of our MVX or Multi-Vector Execution Engine. Figure 11 shows an example of an OS Change Detail report:

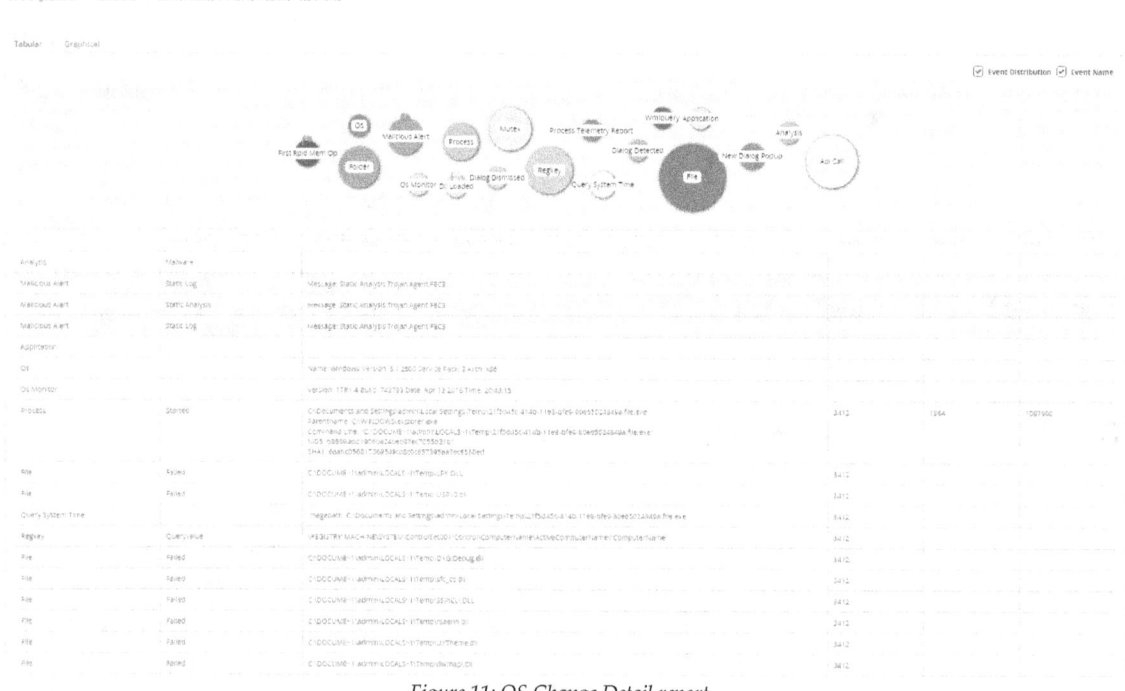

Figure 11: OS Change Detail report

You can see where we document, chronologically, where processes have started or stopped, when files have been created (or when creation attempts have failed), when the system time was queried, when a registry key was detected as being queried at the value level (in the example above, the value is "Computer Name").

FireEye platforms provide downloadable XML. XML is a very malleable and nimble format for data. Although it takes a little work, you can upload the XML into something as simple as Microsoft Excel, and then develop pivot tables or comparisons between two XML data sets to identify deltas. For example, you can use scripts to extract indicators of compromise (IOCs) and display all the file activity in one tab, network IP and ports in another tab, registry values in another tab, mutexes in another tab, as seen in Figure 12. Then you can share the spreadsheet with your third-party or internal endpoint support team:

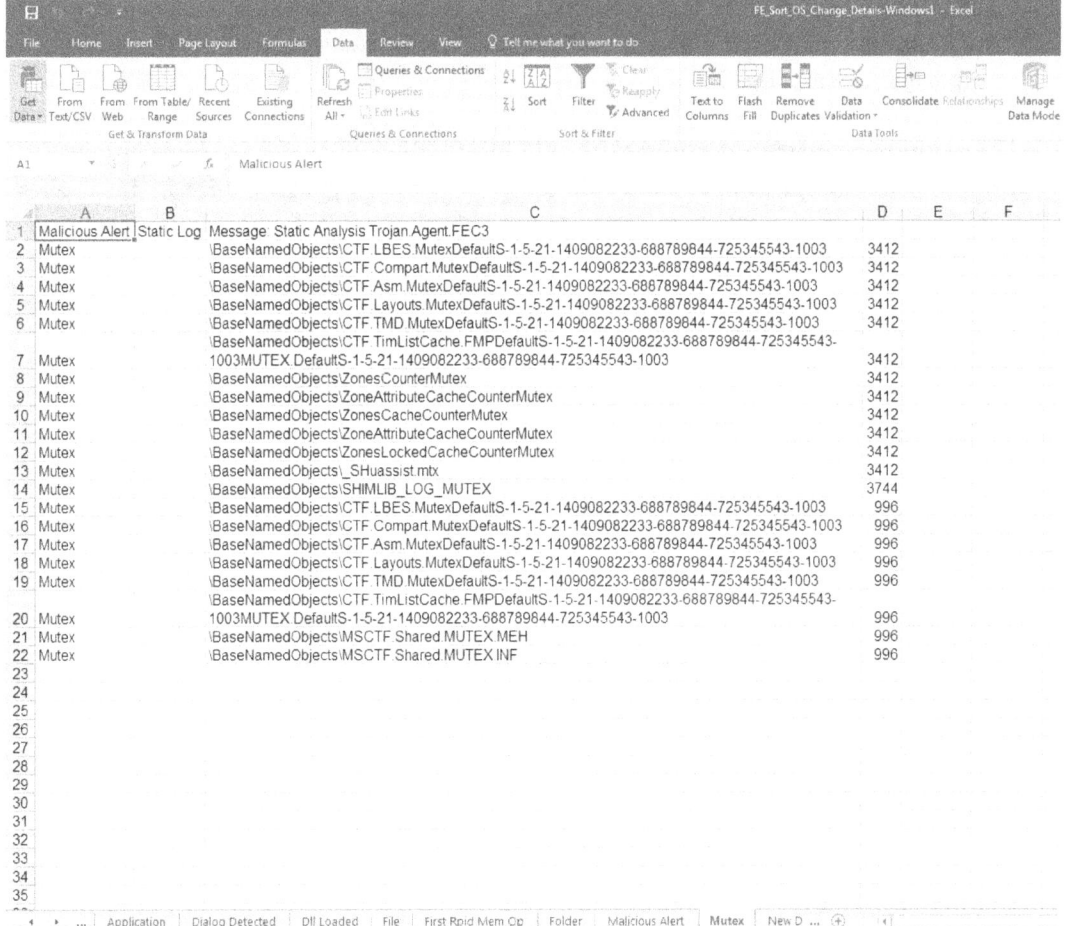

Figure 12: Downloaded XML in Excel

The FireEye Central Management platform (CM Series) can send this data to the Endpoint Security Server (HX Series) in an extended JSON format. The HX creates indicators (called "Rules" in HX 4.5.x) automatically.

Defining Abnormal or Malicious

This goes beyond "I'll know it when I see it". You can most definitely define abnormal: the results of actions or operations that are not expected in normal operation.

For instance, it is normal for a browser to launch Adobe Acrobat Reader—browsers can launch almost any application required for functionality. It is normal for Acrobat Reader to open a PDF. Is it normal for a command prompt to be launched three seconds later and run the file 873af9c543.exe? That is at the least abnormal. PDF files or Acrobat Reader normally don't open command prompts and run executables.

The long-time information security soul in me says this is probably malicious, but that's my first observation and subjective impression. There is an old saying in the legal profession and it applies just as much in cyber security, analytic work and especially forensics: "It doesn't matter what I believe; it only matters what I can prove."

While I might believe 873af9c543.exe is malicious, I have no proof. As an analyst or incident responder, if you want to prove what that .exe is doing, it's time to acquire it, run it in a safe environment (such as a malware lab or virtual host that isn't connected to your physical host or network) and determine what functionality and capabilities it provides.

Threat actors, hackers, and evil doers, while they might be interested in knowing what hardware, operating systems, browsers and applications are included in your various baselines, won't be limited to what you support or have defined as "approved by corporate". On the contrary, they have no limits. There have been many incidents where hackers have used social engineering to have a user install their application or malware on an endpoint . Kevin Mitnick, a security consultant and convicted hacker, has said, "Why spend the time to hack passwords when you can just ask someone and they'll probably tell you?"

In a perfect world, users shouldn't be able to install applications. In the real world, users may know admin passwords or may have inherited admin or higher-level permissions that were never removed. Many engineers, coders and programmers have admin passwords because they so often need to install updates, service packs, development software, and so on.

One way to identify a malicious object is to observe it engaging in what I like to call "the 6 deadly Ds". This will be familiar to many of you that have military or defense contracting experience. Look for the following things:

- Deterioration
- Degradation
- Denial
- Disruption
- Damage
- Destruction

However, malware and the context in which it's run can be more complicated. For instance, data exfiltration is not on the list, but it is a goal of many insider threats, espionage campaigns, and nation-state intrusions.

Using External Resources for Object and Malware Analysis

A common practice is to research indicators of compromise using external sources. For instance, let's say you ran a file folder and filename collection and capture resource on a virtual image taken from a potentially compromised endpoint. When you compare the files and folders of this variable against your known, clean control, this is revealed as a delta or change:

```
C:\Documents and Settings\admin\Local
Settings\Temp\H8563f34fR_7T45Basd35S4E\DePass_Micro.exe
```

Now you want to know what DePass_Micro.exe is and what others have detected or observed about it. You might run the filename or (if you have it) a MD5 or SHA-1 value through a resource like VirusTotal. VirusTotal reports the following (Figure 13):

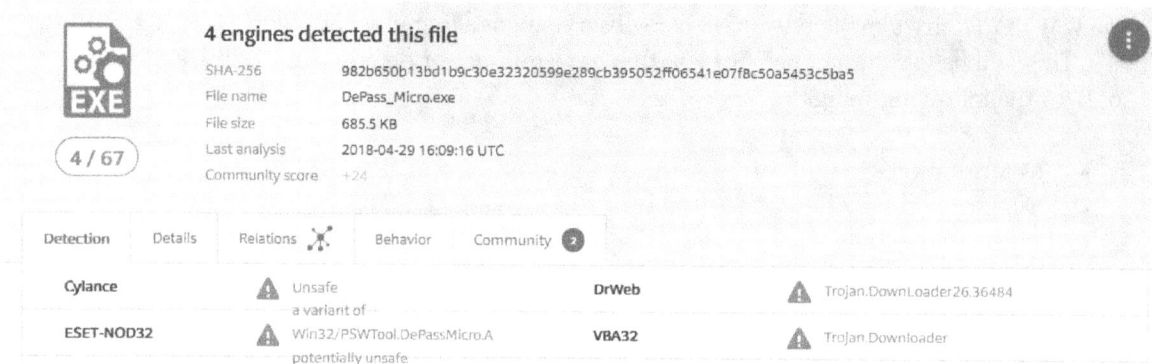

Figure 13: VirusTotal report

As of April 29, 2018, 4 out of 67 virus engines reported that DePass_Micro.exe was a malicious or potentially unsafe executable.

Unfortunately, online resources like this may leave questions unanswered, and they pose some very big risks.

Threat actors can see you. Uploading anything outside your organization is like shooting a flare into the sky. Threat actors and hackers monitor sites like VirusTotal, MetaDefender, VirusCheckmate, and so on. It's highly recommended to use public and Internet-wide resources only when *you don't care whether anyone is watching*. A few online resources even retain search terms such as MD5 values or files names.

Results depend on other submissions. On the day you submit an object, 0 out of 67 virus engines sites may report the object as malicious. Seven days later, all 67 virus engines might report it as malicious. But you won't know unless you check back repeatedly. Detection may also be low if you submit targeted or focused operation malware that isn't generally available.

You may inadvertently exfiltrate sensitive data. Malware droppers and payload objects can be designed to capture troves of data, which is not always deleted after they are submitted. Droppers and payloads submitted to online resources have been found to contain thousands of credentials such as user names, passwords, tokens or passkeys along with IP addresses, hostnames, and personally identifiable information. Threat actors can buy subscription access to online resources that allow them to download any of the objects that have been submitted to that site. If you can't crack open malware objects to clean or sanitize them before you submit them to an external resource, you won't know when you've exposed private data.

Exfiltration can happen in several ways. For example, you may need to send a malware object from one location to another. Your corporate email security detection resources will probably detect and quarantine the object, so you make a snap decision to send it through a free mail service such as yahoo.com, gmail.com, or hotmail.com. Your email provider is likely to detect the malicious object, extract it from your email and submit it as part of their security processes. Many security researchers have noted that this happens with all attachments sent through gmail.com.

Online resources are valuable, as long as you understand the inherent operational risks. It's best to use them only when *you don't mind losing control* of the data you submit.

We are so resource constrained in information security that we can rarely do more than detect intrusions, do some minor of analysis or scoping, stop the pain and kick out the intruder. If you had more time and resources, you might work on a control vs. variable project and pass it to two or three colleagues, who would work on it with a slightly different path or approach. This is a popular military, scientific and academic technique. Although this takes longer, when you can compare notes and consider other input, your observations and conclusions may change dramatically. But no matter how limited your time is limited and how narrow your goals, it is essential and worthwhile to know and learn normal.

Chapter 3: SECOPS Is Required

Anyone who has worked for an information security or cyber security organization will tell you that the security organization doesn't mix well with other groups. Over the past decade, collaboration and integration between information technology and security have gotten somewhat better, but there is still a lot to be desired.

Just as DEVOPS (development operations) is a fusion between your developers and your IT operations, SECOPS (security operations) can be described as a fusion between security and your IT operations. But if you ask different people what SECOPS means, you'll get different answers. To some, SECOPS is ensuring that your information security organization has visibility from the ground up when new systems, applications, infrastructure or resources are introduced into your IT environment. To others, it means actively pursuing security education and culture throughout the operations of the company.

I define SECOPS as integration at the machine level. SECOPS at this level is needed if we ever hope to get a handle on the level of noise that most security teams must deal with daily.

Many outside the information security field don't give security the attention it deserves. Whether in the military or the commercial world, DEVOPS is put first. The focus is on building an infrastructure to support the business or the military command. SECOPS is "nice to have". As a defense contractor, business consultant, and professional trainer, I've seen and heard many horror stories of what has happened when SECOPS is lacking in an organization. This chapter explains the three levels of SECOPS, provides examples and use cases, and discusses some challenges to scaling SECOPS as organizations grow.

Three Levels of SECOPS

I break SECOPS into three levels: organizational, human, and machine. These levels are all difficult. Many organizations and companies have a decent handle on the human level; most struggle with the machine level. We'll look at all three levels. As with all topics and chapters in this book, I'd love to hear feedback about how you accomplish security operations across your own organization.

The Organizational Level

Security operations at an organizational level is how you integrate security across all of the organizations that you interact with. Many will think of integrating SECOPS across internal organizations. In fact, many of the breaches, compromises, intrusions and incidents that I've worked on have their root cause *outside* the organization.

Organizational level security operations should include the following external players:

- Vendors
- Contractors
- Third-party organizations you interact with on a business-to-business (B2B) level
- Support affiliates
- Suppliers
- Consultants

I've seen many organizations—-military, government organizations, global companies—that have extremely organized physical and information security. Penetrating an organization that has such tight security might be as easy as thinking out of the box. For instance, attacking a user at home, by accessing personal email from their local internet service provider, might be easier than attacking them at work on a highly secured network.

One organization had a global, corporate-wide intrusion resulting in a data breach large enough to impact their company for years. The intrusion was started by compromising an associated network that was owned by a contracted third-party organization.

Another organization was compromised by an intrusion-problem set (an advanced persistent threat, or APT) that started with a phishing email that appeared to come from a staffing company with which the organization had a contractor relationship. A screenshot of the email can be seen on many websites (Figure 14).

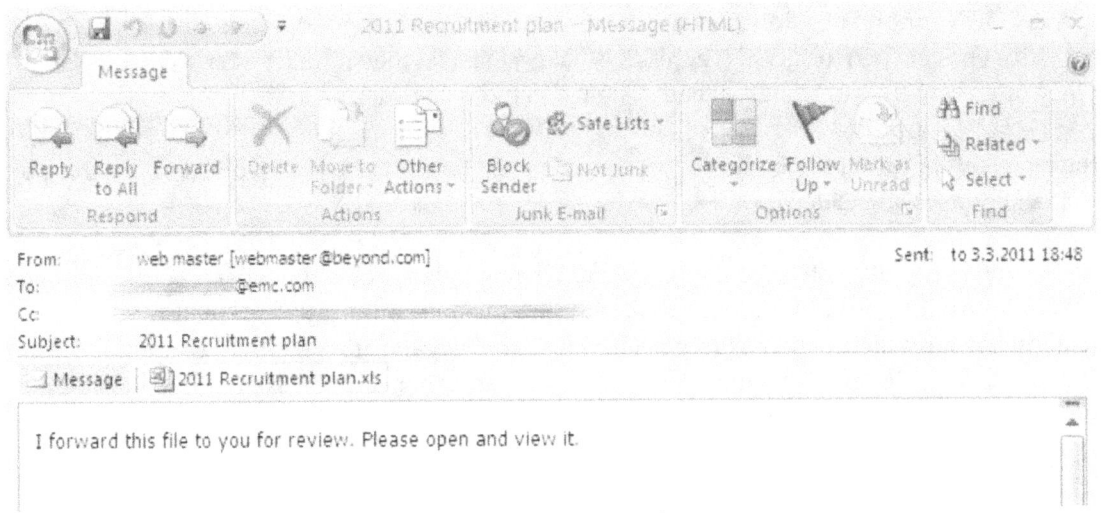

Figure 14: Phishing email

The originator of the email appeared to be Beyond.com—one of the staffing companies that had a relationship with the targeted organization.

In many cases, when a fortress seems impenetrable or the risk is too high, the threat actor may elect for "threat displacement". With threat displacement, the attacker targets a less risky organization that has a weaker defensive posture, such as a third-party contractor.

At the time of the breach shown in Figure 14, in August 2011, I was working as a cyber security analyst for Northrop Grumman in Kuwait. The customer wanted to know whether they were susceptible to the same type of threat. The bottom line was yes, because email headers couldn't (and still can't) be trusted. What we recommended to reduce the risk was to attach a tag that read **[EXTERNAL]** to the actual email address on all email that originated outside the customer's domain. While that won't stop all malicious emails from being opened, it makes the receiver pause for a moment and allows them to identify quickly whether the email was generated by an internal user.

This situation crosses into SECOPS at the human level. If the recipients of the email above had not double-clicked on the attachment and instead had validated whether their contact at the staffing organization had sent the spreadsheet, the outcome of that attack might have been very different. I say, "might have been" because intrusion-problem set threat actors are persistent; if they can't get in one way, they won't give up. Practically, we can't expect users to verify or validate every email and attachment they receive; some senior directors and vice-presidents get 400 – 600 emails (or more) daily.

Evaluate how your organization interfaces with vendors, contractors, suppliers, and so on. Do they have virtual private network (VPN) access? What systems do they interact with? What websites do they interact with, and what backend systems do those websites tie into?

If the recipients of the email above had been suspicious, they might have involved IS. At this point, the email becomes an incident.

When incidents involve both your company and what appears to be a third-party contractor, what are the rules of engagement for interaction? Is the interaction a one-way mode, where you share threat intel, relative alerts, and incident details from your organization to your vendors, suppliers, and contractors? Is it a two-way mode, where your organization and the external organizations share and communicate about threat intel and incident details?

For some of you, there may be no sharing or at best ad hoc, informal communications that sometimes happen, sometimes don't. For instance, maybe some threat intel is shared but there is agreement to share alert or incident details. Service-level agreements or statements of work may preclude you from sharing any information at all. However, the more information you can share between organizations, the more tightly you can integrate SECOPS at an organizational level, and the better off you'll be on multiple levels. (Just as your mom and dad told you when you were little, "Sharing is caring".)

The FireEye Network Security, Email Security, FX, AX, Endpoint Security and CM platforms can integrate with the FireEye Dynamic Threat Intelligence cloud. To facilitate different levels of integration, FireEye offers one-way and two-way licensing. One-way licensing is a "receive only" mode where a customer can receive intelligence from the DTI cloud, but does not send anything up to the cloud. Although that is a secure way of integrating, it doesn't help the community in general and therefore costs more. With two-way licensing, customers receive intel from the DTI cloud and send certain types of non-identifying data and telemetry up to the cloud, enabling many customers to share threat information safely.

The Human Level

Most organizations can implement SECOPS at the human level most easily. Your organization most likely already has moderate levels of human SECOPS among supervisors, team leads, managers, site leads, and so on in intra-company or cross-departmental meetings. However, meetings don't provide the flexibility or the freedom with which a tier 2 or 3 analyst or incident responder can walk over to the system administrators to ask questions or talk for a few minutes. Many false positives, false negatives, anomalies and abnormalities can be run to ground just by asking a few key questions of the right people.

In some organizations, security analysts and sysadmins aren't on the same floor, in the same building or even on the same continent. I've worked for organizations where as soon as I called someone in TECHOPS or WANOPS and said, "Hi, this is Chris with Information Security", they virtually shut down. In other organizations, calling or even emailing someone was not standard protocol. The method of communication traversed the corporate structure. If you were on the security team, you would bring your question or issue to your team's site lead. The site lead would refer to a big book that held various contractors' statements of work and tasking orders, identify the right contractor to address your question or issue, and forward your question to that contractor's site lead.

One of the best resources any IS team can have is a member who came from another group in your organization. Someone who spent years on a server administration team and crossed over to information security brings institutional or tribal knowledge with them. When an incident occurs, that person's old colleagues, friends and associates can be quickly called upon, either formally or informally.

Another example of SECOPS at the human level is your end users. Hopefully, your end users are not afraid to interact with the IS team. I've asked this question while teaching many times: "What is one of the largest detection grids that you currently have deployed?". Sometimes the answers are along the lines of "That would be our primary IDS grid with 4 servers, roughly 20 sensors per network, coverage with over 1,500 signatures grouped into various categories such as denial of service attack detection or http protocol detection anomalies, etc."

What I rarely hear, especially from the more technically oriented students, is: "Our largest detection grid is our end users".

Your end users are the front lines. Maybe they wouldn't reach out to you directly but when they sense something is wrong, they should feel comfortable enough to reach out to the service desk, desktop support or someone that can get to you. End users should not be reluctant to bring something up because they fear being blamed for doing something wrong.

The better your organization is in integrating human interaction with security operations, the better your professional life will be. It's extremely easy to get wrapped up in the technical side of events, alerts, alarms, thresholds, signatures, definitions, access control lists, indicators of compromise, and so on. There will always be a human component on both the attacker side and the victim side of every breach. The more human information you have, the better you will be able to answer critical questions.

The Machine Level

Most organizations struggle with SECOPS at the machine level. It's a critical component to help reduce noise, non-actionable events or alerts, and false positives generated from known conditions. Within the past year an entire industry has developed to get security platforms and products to talk to other security platforms and products. The whole of Chapter 7 is dedicated to the subject of security operations, automation and response.

SECOPS at the machine level is the fusion of IT resources directly with IS resources. Currently, it's frequently done with a mashup of Perl, Ruby, or Python scripts that can take advantage of APIs (application programming interfaces).

Not all APIs provide all types of functionality, but with most, you can GET (request) information and PUT or POST (update or create) data. A popular form of API within FireEye is the REST API. If you're lucky, your API will be documented. If not, you'll have your work cut out for you.

Before Mandiant was acquired by FireEye in 2014, we did a lot of work with MIR (Mandiant Intelligent Response) controllers using the MIR API. The API on MIR was not documented well at all. We basically put a sniffer inline between the MIR thick client/console and the controller, uploaded SSL certificates from the MIR controller to the sniffer and recorded everything that happened between the client and the server. Then we picked apart packets and commands so we could effectively script and use the API. This was over six years ago, which is almost a geologic age in the information security business. (FireEye has very well documented APIs now and our customers can script operations without pain.)

This example highlights the level of effort that may be required when you need to virtually wire together IS and IT resources but you only have a poorly documented API. It is challenging to integrate them effectively and I rarely see this type of integration accomplished.

The Biggest Challenge for Machine SECOPS

The first and greatest challenge to implementing machine SECOPS is the sheer volume of events. Though many organizations don't recognize it, there is a moderate to high potential that your security operations center or team is facing an almost insurmountable mathematical problem.

Take the average number of alerts, alarms, events and incident details that you receive daily from all your detection, defensive and protection resources. Divide it by the number of analysts you have working those events. While this formula is not exact, it gives you an idea of the scale of your mathematical challenges to security operations. The following example shows the scale of the problem along with some ideas for addressing it.

Scenario: Machine SECOPS in an Enterprise Organization

This scenario shows a large, global, enterprise-level customer with the following characteristics:

- 425,000 endpoints
- Endpoints span 4 different networks:
    - Production
    - Supervisory control and data acquisition (SCADA)
    - Research and development
    - Corporate classified
- Average number of daily events across all four networks that require screening, assessment and triaging: 3.1 million
- Number of full-time analysts covering 24 hours, 7 days a week, 365 days a year: 18 (9 per 12-hour shift)

The base formula is:
    18 analysts ÷ 3.1 million events = 172,222 events per day (EPD)

For simplicity, let's assume that the 172,222 EPD are evenly divided between shifts:
    9 analysts ÷ 86,111 events per shift = 9,568 events per shift, per analyst
    9,568 events ÷ 12 hours = 797 events per hour (EPH)
    797 EPH ÷ 60 minutes = 13 EPM (events per minute)

A single analyst taking no breaks, never needing to eat, check email, attend meetings, document the work or do anything but stare at a screen for 12 hours, would need to make decisions about 13 events per minute.

Now what happens when that analyst notices a single event that requires more than 4.6 seconds of time?

Event Volume Leads to False Positives

Our enterprise customer uses Microsoft Active Directory (AD) Sites and Services. Let's consider the following scenario. Your IDS trips an alert that looks something like this:

"Attempted DDoS detected directed at interface 1 on Server DC-DNS-BLDG5FLR3"

As an analyst, you start investigating that alert. Instead of taking the alert at its face value, you apply SECOPS at the human level first. You try to ask your AD admin if anything unusual is going on with Server DC-DNS in Building 5, 3rd floor. But the admin is absent today—you're on your own.

You run a packet sniffer on the subnet DC-DNS-BLDG5FLR3 is on and you notice a high level of LDAP BIND requests, as seen in Figure 15:

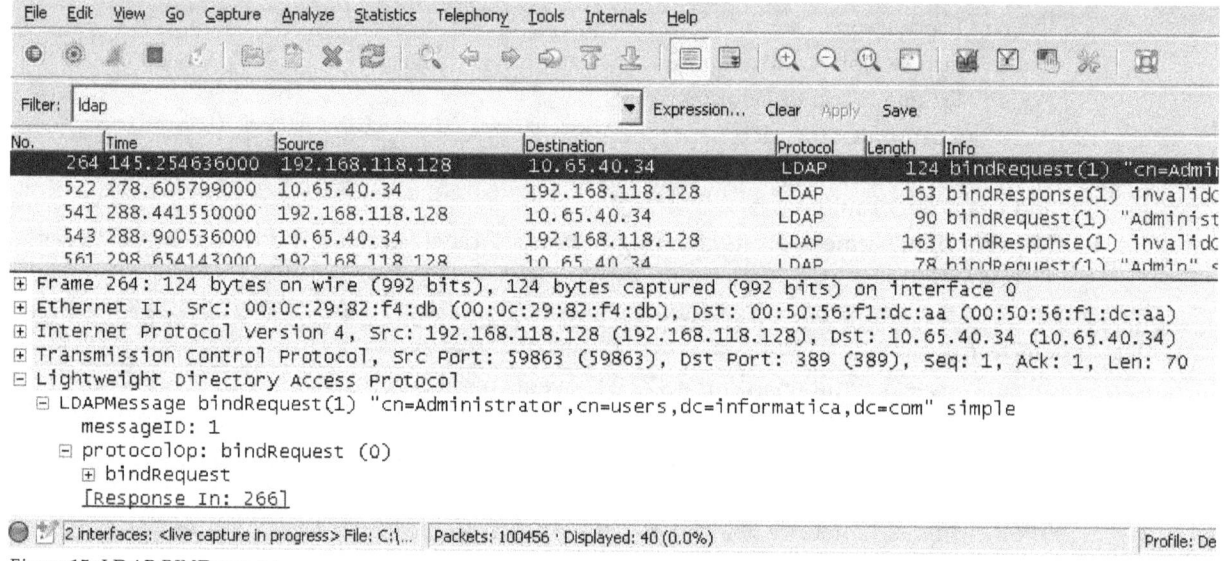

Figure 15: LDAP BIND requests

In a case like this, you're already starting down a road that could probably be avoided by having context. It depends on how familiar you are with the traffic in the packet capture. You may need to investigate each LDAP BIND request to determine if it is normal, benign or malicious.

We'll shortcut the context required for now and reveal that the alert ultimately turns out to be a false positive. The root cause was an authorized service interruption (ASI) when the WAN operations team took a WAN link down for maintenance. In response to this condition, Active Directory Sites and Services generated excessive replication monitoring and status traffic packets, which the IDS interpreted as an attempted distributed denial of service (DDOS) event

SECOPS at a machine level could have prevented this false positive if the IDS was wired into Active Directory Sites and Services replication-level events.

Machine SECOPS Prevents the False Positive Scenario

Figure 16 shows Active Directory Sites and Services built upon three network links between Indianapolis, Chicago and Atlanta in the United States:

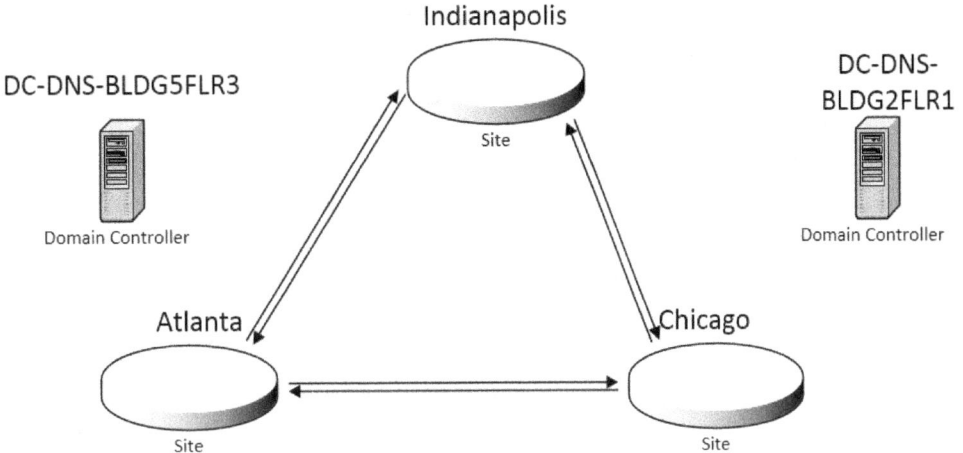

Figure 16: AD network links

Services running over those sites include DNS, LDAP, FTP, and so on.

The IDS alert was generated because the site link between Indianapolis and Atlanta, IND-ATL, went down.

Active Directory has a component for replication. When the site link goes down, DC-DNS-BLDG5FLR3 can still communicate with DC-DNS-BLDG2FLR1. Both domain controllers will communicate over IND-CHI and then CHI-ATL, redirecting replication around IND-ATL.

Now let's add IDS sensors to the network (Figure 17):

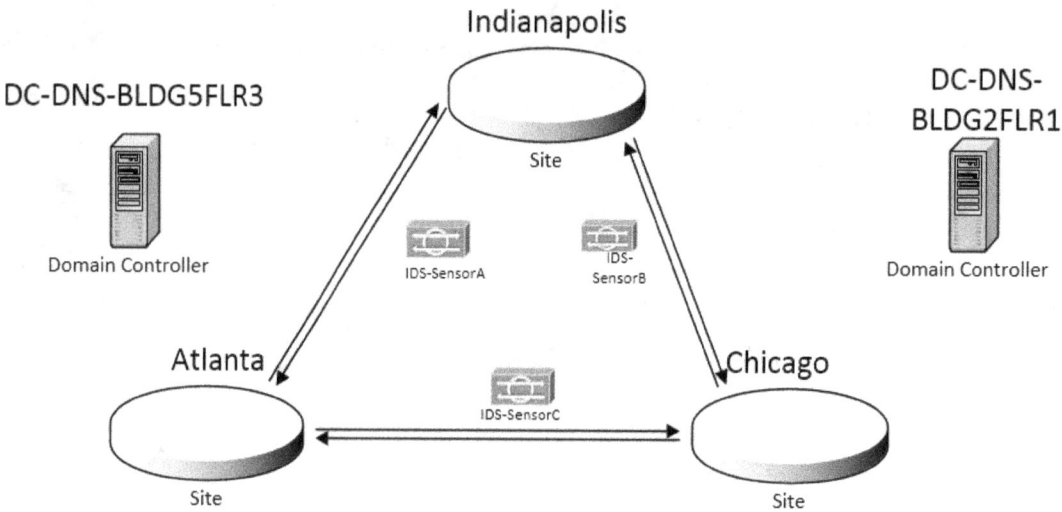

Figure 17: Network with IDS sensors

IDS-SensorA detected the ASI and interpreted it as a DDOS attack. Why? Because the Microsoft Replication Monitor (REPLMON) running across all domain controllers constantly checks the status of link functionality. As the IND-ATL comes back up, that replication route will be returned to active but until then, REPLMON will continue to monitor status of the link. That's normal for Active Directory. Unfortunately, the IDS sensors and the upstream management server are not integrated with Active Directory Sites and Services running on DC-DNS-BLDG5FLR3 or the other domain controllers.

If AD and the IDS management system were integrated and the right API calls were in place, they could communicate with one another to provide network-level context. The IDS management system could isolate a service interruption to the relevant sensor (IDS-SensorA) and temporarily disable or quiet relative signatures while the authorized service interruption is active. The false positive alert would never fire. Plenty of IDS resources integrate with AD Users and Computers for access and authentication. However, I'm not aware of any that integrate AD Sites and Services replication monitoring with an IDS management system.

I've worked with many IDS resources for years, including Snort, Suricata, McAfee IDS, Cisco's commercial IDS/SourceFire, and the FireEye Network Security Platform, among others. All of them contain their signatures in a .conf file, and that entire file is either enabled or disabled. But imagine that an IDS signature (or set of signatures) could be configured with a time-to-live (TTL) value that could be dynamically adjusted by an IDS signature management system. The signature could be disabled when a change of state is received from the management server, and reenabled when the management server sends an "enable" signal.

Dynamic Virtualization and SECOPS

If you think that SECOPS at a machine level is difficult, you probably don't want to hear what issues dynamic virtualization creates with security operations. Dynamic virtualization and cloud providers like Amazon, Microsoft, Google, and Oracle are rapidly increasing the scope provided for platforms and services in our information technology infrastructure. Virtual machines, personal computers, platforms, operating systems and applications can be spun up or terminated in seconds to minutes.

Many security architects and engineers cringe when they hear "seconds to minutes." It's hard enough to engineer solutions, determine sensor placement, and compute statistics around protocol coverage and communication in "weeks to months".

Virtualization and the cloud can be agile and flexible and can scale upward, to the advantage of Information Technology organizations but to the detriment of Information Security organizations. Our firewalls are groaning under the load of application or protocol dissection compounded by virtualization, detection grids that include host-based resources or endpoint-based resources, and network security devices that were architected well before the rise of cloud and virtualization.

For security operations execution, we must have the right telemetry, detection and protection mechanisms in place for visibility throughout the physical environment, the virtual and cloud environments and a hybrid of both. When considering cloud and dynamic virtualization, make sure you know where the entry and exit points are on your network for those providers. Chapter 9 addresses cloud providers in depth.

Use Cases Where Lack of SECOPS Caused Issues

This section summarizes a few notable use cases where integration or a fusion between IT and IS resources would have prevented burning of analytic resources, time, and money. These use cases demonstrate what I call RTA or Reactionary Traffic Alarms. Security products and platforms typically don't differentiate between alerts or events and RTA. Security operations teams often need to apply their human analytic and contextual knowledge to determine whether an alarm or alert they are looking at is caused by something other than a genuinely intrusive event that should be wrapped into an incident.

In the example in the previous section, the alerts were a reaction to a link service outage that appeared to be a DDoS attack. Here are a few others:

- An in-path routing device fails, interrupting network connectivity. Several endpoints are no longer available. ICMP replies with "destination unreachable" responses. The high volume of responses is interpreted as an ICMP flood by IDS, IPS, and packet capture devices that are running event correlation or Suricata rules. A false positive alert is generated in reaction to single equipment failure.

- Someone uses replication mechanisms or protocols inadvertently, or without consideration for the detection and monitoring resources inline with the network. Abnormal characteristics of the protocols or replication components appear to be out of specification and thus trigger alerts. This false positive occurs because context and applied correlation are lacking.

  True story: I once worked with a newly minted MCSE who had just gotten his security clearance. He knew he was going to be sent to a forward COB (Combat Operating Base) and was not allowed to bring in any type of removable media. He also knew that all domain controllers had a directory called C:\Windows\NTDS, which contained a file called NTDS.DIT, which Active Directory replication had to synchronize across all domain controllers. (NTDS.DIT is the NT Directory Services.Directory Information Tree.) So he zipped the current season of a popular reality TV show into a file called NTDS1.ZIP and dropped it into that folder. He expected that by the time he arrived at the forward COB, his TV show would be there waiting for him. What he didn't know was that AD replication was designed for data objects much smaller than compressed media files. The attempt to replicate his enormous file across all controllers brought AD replication to its knees. Security analysts jumped in to investigate the "malicious threat actor" that was using AD replication inappropriately. It ended up being a career-ending move for that young MCSE.

- In a variation on authorized service interruptions, servers are taken offline for patching, service packs, or maintenance without coordination between server admins and security operations. Endpoint Agents lose connectivity to their servers. A dramatic loss in EPS and polling failures from the agents result.

- An analyst sees logs entries going to a suspicious-looking domain. To check what IP address that translates to, the analyst runs nslookup on the domain. The domain matches an entry on the domain blacklist, and Domain Matching alerts are generated. The alerts are a reaction to analyzing an incident on the same network where the incident, compromise or breach occurred

The last case is a frequent in-house security operations issue. Unfortunately, not many organizations can afford a separate domain for security analysis or network defense.

Challenges Scaling SECOPS

A major challenge to SECOPs is scaling as an organization grows. Integration and collaboration tend to be highest when an organization is small. In a very tight, closely working group of professionals, communication between DEVOPS and SECOPS will be informal and natural. Even medium-sized organizations will have a better SECOPS at the human level than a large enterprise organization. As an organization grows, many variables muddy the waters.

For example, let's say your organization is a worldwide logistics company that has grown fast because of mergers and acquisitions made in various regions of the world. Management decides to create an enterprise information security (EIS) group that provides policy, strategic planning and high-level enterprise services such as DNS security and identity and authentication services. More tactical-level security, such as endpoint or network security and issues such as baselines and applications, is left to each country or regional IS group, which is closer to the users. Coordinating SECOPS across the entire global infrastructure of the organization will be very difficult because of different time zones, languages, user demographics, legal requirements, and turf battles.

Integrating SECOPS at a technical level between your security detection, defensive and protection resources and IT resources will be an uphill battle, but it's one that needs to be fought.

Chapter 4: Detection Methodologies

I've had many bosses who have said, "Don't just bring me a problem—bring me at least 2 or 3 alternatives and recommendations". With that in mind, at the end of the chapter, I provide a few recommendations to consider. One reason I wrote this book is to bring up topics that I wish old-timers had told me early when I started a career in Information Security. Alert saturation and event fatigue are very real issues that rarely get discussed.

A few industry security companies believe that the more alerts their products generate, the more valuable they are to their customers. Nothing could be further from the truth. In cyber security, more is not better. We're already buried under an avalanche of alerts, events, alarms, packets, exploits, threat intelligence, incidents, intrusions, breaches, compromises, and the list goes on and on.

I've taught for many customers that have what they call "dirty nets", or, more formally "guest networks". When guests arrive and shuffle into conference rooms, when contractors are onsite and need the internet but are not allowed to connect to the production network, when vendors arrive and need an internet connection, the guest WiFi or LAN ports are standing at the ready. A few of those customers don't even consume alerts or security information from their dirty nets. The guest network is like swimming in a pool with no lifeguard—use at your own risk. They have enough challenges staying on top of the production networks they are tasked with protecting. I'm not sure if I agree with that strategy but when I travel to teach, I'm a visitor and riding their dirty net—so detection, defense and protection are on me (or my employer).

Your detection methodologies must be as diverse as all the threats that you need to detect and all the resources the security operations team is responsible for covering. Many would say, "That's easy—we have signatures and behavioral based detection methods. End of story." It's never "end of story". If it were, we would have had this entire business of defending and protecting networks and endpoints so well covered, there would never be another hack, intrusion, breach or compromise again.

Key Factors

Level of Control

One key question to ask is: how does your organization maintain security on endpoints that roam off your network? For most organizations, that answer typically falls into one of three categories (or a mix):

- **FULL CONTROL:** We maintain full control of our agents, applications and security resources at all times on all endpoints, both internal (within the corporate intranet) and external (connected remotely through the internet).
- **PARTIAL CONTROL:** We maintain full control of our agents, applications and security resources at all times on internal endpoints. We can maintain a subset of functionality but do not have full control of our security resources on external endpoints.
- **NO CONTROL:** While an endpoint is on our network, we have full control. When an endpoint roams off the network, we have no control of our security resources.

Typically, students in FireEye training are covered under full control if they have HX primary and HX DMZ controllers. However, we also do training for companies that have earlier models of Network Security and Email Security platforms centrally managed by a CM platform. Some customers have another resource for their endpoints – parts of the Department of Defense have used Host Based Security System (HBSS) resources for years (HBSS is a suite of McAfee applications).

The next thing to consider, even if you think your organization falls into the "full control" bucket, is: how much control do you have when an endpoint is in specific states? States such as:

- Power on, plugged in
- Power on, battery connected
- Suspension or hibernation mode
- Power off
- Connected to VPN
- Disconnected from VPN

Let's say your security team needs to take a memory image across a group of endpoints that are point-of-sale devices. No problem for the devices that are powered on, plugged in, fully operational and currently connected. What about the devices that are in a time zone across the globe, and are in suspension or hibernation mode because it's considered off hours where they are? Some would reason that if an endpoint is in a suspension or hibernation mode, so is the malware. However, many malware droppers have trigger mechanisms that fire when the endpoint comes out of hibernation or reboots.

Trust but Verify—Simulation and Testing

Your detection methodologies and specific capabilities must be simulated and tested in your organization. If you are away from the front lines and are in a supervisory or management role, you may be told that you have various detection methods covered, but how has that been validated? Can you verify that?

Consider the importance of flight simulators. Periodically, airplane pilots are taken off active flight duty status and spend a week or more going through flight simulations to ensure they are up to date with tactics, techniques and procedures. They know they can handle an engine fire or hydraulic failure because they have simulated it and validated that they can work it.

Penetration testing is a step in the right direction, but you might be surprised to know how many pen testers don't use malware or depend on errors or failures. In fact, some penetration testers are bound or restricted by rules of engagement (ROEs) where certain resources or targets may be off limits.

You need a lab. You need the malware. You need a replication of your production detection and protection resources, and you need packet replay capability. These are not easy to acquire and require budget and resources (and time) for lab work. You also need current and sustainment training, which could range from instructor-led classroom training to cyber range and qualification training.

When new malware is reported, the first question should be whether you can detect it. The next question should be about how you validate or verify that detection. In prior positions I've held as an analyst team lead, I knew my team cringed when I asked whether we could do "VV" (validate and verify). They knew they had their work cut out for them. They also knew that in the end, we would have a solid confirmation of yes, we can or no, we can't.

If the answer was "No, we can't detect this", of course the next question was "What do we need to do to detect this in the future?" Technically, that would branch to other questions and briefing points that related to risk levels, compensating controls, exposure factors, and so on. Depending on your environment, you may not be required to detect every type of malware or threat that comes across the news wires.

One organization that I worked for drew the line at forensics. If we needed to forensically analyze a hard drive, we would collect the hard drive, image it, hash the image, and send it to a specialized forensics group. Another US military organization that I supported in Stuttgart, Germany did not allow contractors to perform forensic analysis. That type of analysis was handled by a team of government-service civilians. Analysts often came across issues related to counterintelligence and law enforcement and sometimes were required to testify in court cases. That organization did not want to put a contractor in the position of being required to testify on behalf of the government or the US military.

The next sections discuss types of detection methodologies.

Signature-Based Detection

Our entire industry was built on signature-based detection. Though a few proclaim that signature-based detection is dead, I don't think that we'll ever get away from it completely. Without signature-based resources—firewalls, IDS, IPS, anti-virus, anti-malware, proxies—the noise level of objects that analysts contend with would be overwhelming.

Various vendors have different names for their signatures. FireEye, relies heavily on Indicators of Compromise (IOCs). The OpenIOC format was defined by Mandiant field-level consultants. Other names for IOCs include artifacts, objects, signatures, definitions, and so on.

An IOC looks something like Figure 18:

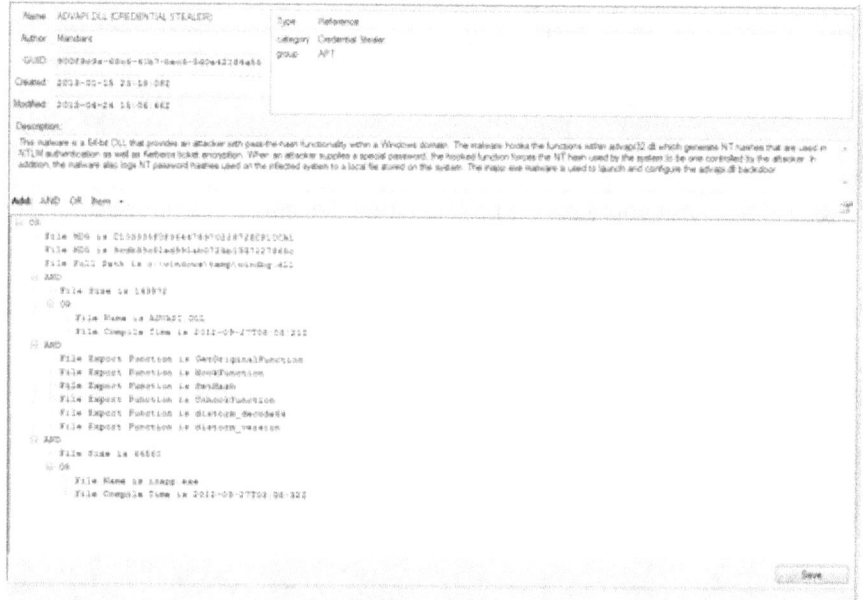

Figure 18: IOC example

This indicator came from an IOC set from 2015 and was categorized as a credential stealer. The updated IOC editor facilitates conditions that include more operators, such as "less than", "greater than", "starts with", "ends with", and so on.

Snort or Suricata signatures look something like this:

```
alert tcp $EXTERNAL_NET any -> $SQL_SERVERS 1443 (msg:"SQL brute force
login attempt"; flow:to_server,established; content:"|02|"; depth:1;
offset:39; nocase; detection_filter; track by_src, count 5, seconds;
reference:redacted; classtype:suspicious-loging; sid:99999;rev:8)
```

YARA Malware Framework rules look something like this:

```
Rule KINS_dropper {
        Meta:
                    author = "Chris-BigBiz from FireEye Products and Platforms
Training - Customer Success"
                    description = "Matching protocol, process injects and windows
exploits used in KINS dropper"
                    weight = 90
        strings:
                    // Network protocol
                    $n1 = "tid=%d&ta=%s-%x" fullword
                    $n2 = "fid=%d" fullword
                    //Injects
                    $i0 = "Global\\%s%x"
                    $i1 = "Inject::InjectProcessByName()"
                    $i2 = "Inject::CopyImpageToProcess()"
                    // UAC Bypass
                    $uac1 = "ExploitMS10_092"
                    $uac2 = \\globalroot\\systemroot\\system32\\tasks\\ ascii
wide
        condition:
                    2 of ($n*) and 2 of ($i*) and 1 of ($uac*)
}
```

It's not so easy to peek into the exact format of antivirus and anti-malware rules, but Figure 19 shows one from ClamAV running as part of Kali Linux. (ClamAV is open-source, GNU-public license, Linux-based antivirus detection.) In the daily.ndb file, two entries are circled: WIN.Trojan.Lolu and WIN.Trojan.Vobfus. The names of the viruses are in ASCII but the rest of each signature is in hexadecimal.

```
root@kali:~/clamav-0.98.7/database# more daily.ndb
WIN.Trojan.Lolu:1:*:6e236923000000000ffffffff0400000022202f66000000000ffffffff0100
000041000000ffffffff010000004300000000ffffffff07000000636d*6f72644c756369
WIN.Trojan.Vobfus-10289:1:*:3900670073006d00000000000004000000360033000000000000600
0007900680037000000008000000340077007100650000000000004000006066000360000000000004000
00007a0077000000000000600000063006a00310000000600000073003100026000000006000000320000
62006400660006a007900670070000000040000007900390000000000004000000650073000000000002000
00002c0000004000000656078
WIN.Trojan.Vobfus-10290:1:*:7700670007a000000066000000007500700078000000006000000070000
7600740000000080000000630062007500720000000004000000750079000000000040000007400
64000000000000a000006e0079006e00630072000000001000000063006500076006100730006b006600
6900000000000000c00000007900
```

Signature-based detection helps with object weighting and overall product performance, speeding up the detection process. If we detect with high confidence that an object is a known piece of malware, we do not need to continue with dynamic analysis. The dynamic analysis engines are not overrun with objects and are available for in-depth work. FireEye Network Security (NX), Email Security (EX), File Security (FX) and Malware Analysis (AX) platforms all have static analysis, signature-based engines (along with other dynamic and proprietary detection engines).

Overreliance on signature-based detection can be a failure point. Front-line, hands-on security operations teams have direct experience with the challenges inherent in signature-based detection, although higher levels of management in IS or IT may not. Traditional anti-virus and anti-malware detection is inadequate for sophisticated nation-state APT threat actors. Some advanced threat actors test their malware against anti-virus and anti-malware products in their own labs.

Signature-based detection doesn't extend to intrusions, compromises, breaches or any incidents in which behavior doesn't match any malware definitions or signatures deployed in your operation. When threat actors use the same tools and resources that your administrators and support staff use, they may not even need to deploy malware. This technique is often referred to as "living off the land".

Pattern-Based Detection

It's rare to find malware that is static in nature. Malware written to evade static detection engines employs dynamic properties in exploits, droppers, and payloads. Malware deployed to one system will not be the same when it is deployed to a second system, third system, and so on. Dropper/payload file names or directories, registry keys or values, port communication, and other conditions may change each time the malware is deployed on a new system. This is typically referred to as *polymorphic malware.* Malware droppers/payloads are known to employ some very tricky mechanisms. Some malware uses variables such as hostnames or IP address octets to compute values that are included in the way they write objects into the registry or determine which port to communicate on. Complete or partial hostnames or IP addresses can become seed values for encryption.

For dynamically changing malware, you can no longer rely on static signatures. You need to match the characteristics or patterns associated with what you are trying to detect.

One way to apply pattern-based detection is to employ regular expressions, or regex. There are various flavors of regex. One that is popular with many of our products and platforms is PCRE or PERL Compatible Regular Expressions. Figure 20 shows an example of a regex condition in one of our HX indicators of compromise:

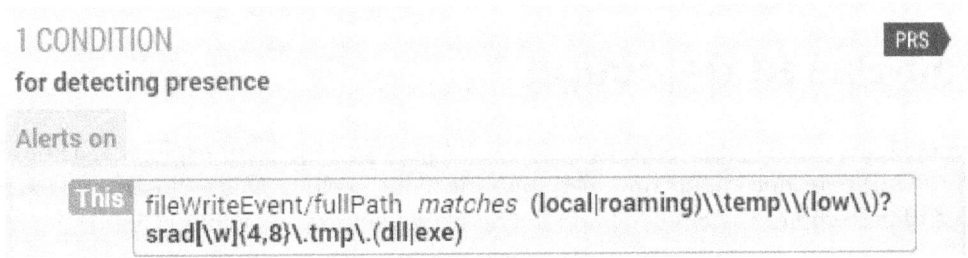

Figure 20: Regex condition in HX IOC

This is also how many Data Leak Prevention (DLP) devices detect leaks that include personally identifiable information (PII), such as telephone numbers, email addresses or Social Security numbers. In the United States, a Social Security number is 3 digits, followed by a dash, 2 digits, followed by another dash, then 4 digits (such as 123-45-6789). The following regular expression matches this pattern:

```
^(\d{3}-?\d{2}\-?\d{4}|xxx-xx-xxxx)$
```

Entire books and websites are dedicated to regular expressions, so I won't dive into those details further.

Other pattern-based detection methods include Verbal Expressions, a library that builds regular expressions from readable code. Lua offers an alternative to regex through C patterns. XML (Extensible Markup Language) can be converted into xFilters that can be evaluated against data. No book can cover all the different patterns and methods.

Even more challenging than writing a pattern-based indicator of compromise, signature or definition is knowing when it is appropriate. For that, you will need to understand the behavior of malware when it is deployed, installed or detonated.

Behavior-Based Detection or Dynamic Analysis

Behavior-based detection or dynamic analysis was FireEye's original specialty and it is still a major part of our technology stack and capabilities. The slogan was, "Detect Zero Days". Zero-day malware is malware that has never been detected before. How do you detect zero-day malware when there are no known signatures, artifacts, objects or definitions? You must let the malware run, observe its behavior, measure it or extract telemetry as it runs, and analyze the behavior to decide whether it is malicious.

Vendors have a variety of methods for dynamic analysis. At FireEye, we call our dynamic analysis engine MVX, for Multi-Vector Execution engine. Other vendors refer to this type of functionality as sandboxing. No two sandboxes are the same, and some are more easily evaded than others.

Exploit-Based Detection

Exploit-based detection monitors applications that are popular targets for exploits. If a known exploit is run, the detection engine fires alerts specific to the exploit. This is closely tied to endpoint detection and protection. The FireEye Endpoint Security platform has Exploit Guard.

An example is ransomware. At the time this book is being written, ransomware by itself can't propagate or travel (that could change in the future). All forms of ransomware need to be integrated with a distribution mechanism of some kind. Exploit kits provide that mechanism. Exploit kit activity that has targeted an application, browser or operating system component can be detected based on certain sets of conditions. Once ransomware gains a foothold on an endpoint, once the encryption begins, removal and remediation without paying the ransom can be difficult or impossible. Organizations that want to detect ransomware before it gains a foothold need to be detecting at an exploit level.

This can be tricky. One popular method of exploit detection requires injecting a monitoring DLL into the object that requires monitoring. If the DLL is injected incorrectly or the object doesn't take well to the monitoring injection, that can lead, on a Windows system, to a BSOD (Blue Screen of Death).

Machine Learning–Based Detection

Detection based on machine learning has been developing in the security industry. Machine learning uses data ranges and determines which algorithms to apply. FireEye has multiple examples of machine learning technologies. One is the Dynamic Threat Intelligence Cloud (DTI). Another is Malware Guard on the Endpoint Security platform. Malware Guard applies machine learning detection to portable executable (PE) files to determine the probability that a file is malicious. Malware Guard uses three types of machine learning training—supervised, unsupervised and reinforcement training. FireEye has a distinct advantage in machine learning because of its access to hundreds of millions of Microsoft Windows executables.

Though some call machine learning artificial intelligence, to me, it isn't quite the same. True AI to me means a system that is smart enough to analyze its own environment and make its own decisions and assessments autonomously. I'd love an AI engine that analyzed an IDS signature set against the last two weeks of vulnerability scans, identified detection weaknesses in applications and operating system components, and dynamically created and deployed new signatures to address them. We're still a long way from anything like that in our industry.

Detection Based on Multiple Conditions, Rules and Correlation

This detection method is based on multiple conditions, rule and correlation. A group of conditions or a rule that is defined by a query or correlation conditions can be set to trigger an alert or event. Figure 21 shows one from the FireEye Helix platform:

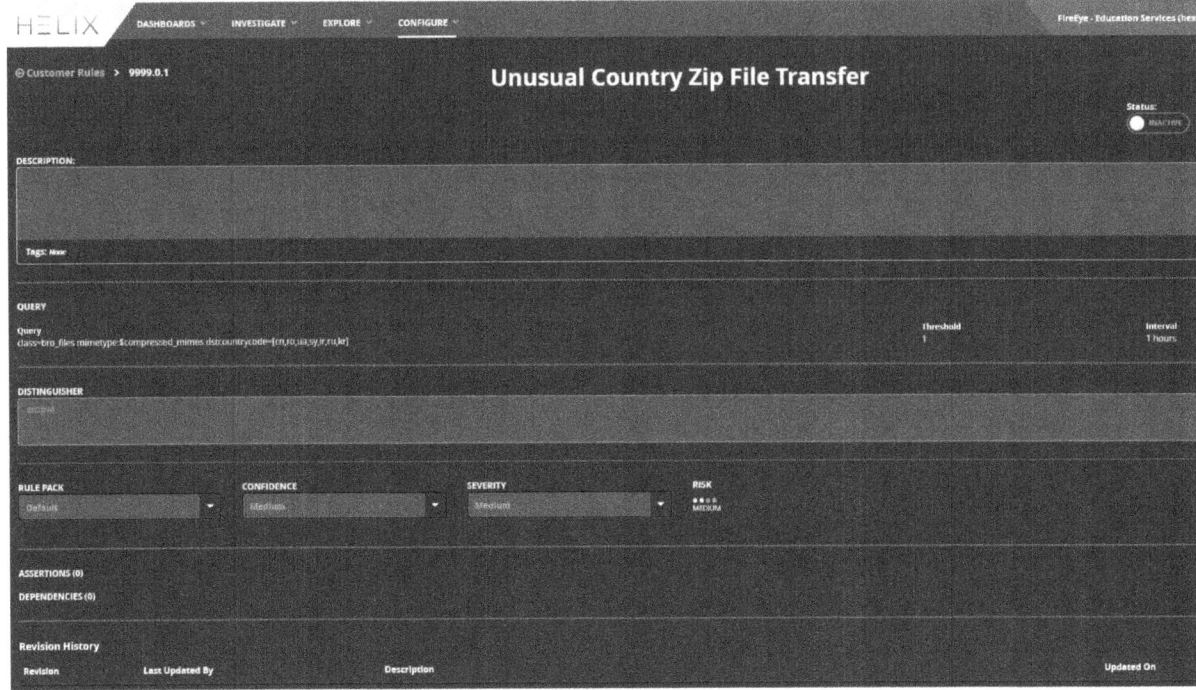

Figure 21: Helix rule based on multiple conditions

In Helix, rules are based on query conditions. The example shows that events captured by bro_files resources will be evaluated for mime files that are compressed and going to destination countries of China, Romania, Ukraine, Syria, Iran, Russia, or South Korea. If your organization has no reason to send compressed mime files to those countries, this rule will generate an alert that should be triaged by an analyst or the security team.

Most security information and event management (SIEM) systems or enterprise security management systems have a way to define correlation conditions to throttle groups of events and possibly trigger an action when certain conditions are met. While it takes some time to learn the rules when setting these up, they can be very effective when you need to tie together multiple conditions or generate rules based on queries that can fire alerts.

Context-Based Detection

Context-based detection means applying outside context to the results of your detection. Adding context is difficult and you can never have enough. The easiest way to add context is not through something quantitative—it's by using your human knowledge, background, history and experience to understand an event. Until we can attach probes to measure your brain waves, this can only be qualitative. The closest thing we have in the technology currently available is correlation-rule-multiple-condition detection; time will tell how accurate machine learning models and algorithms become.

One of the most effective and newest ways to evade even the most accurate of detection engines isn't to introduce malware. It's the creative use of built-in or administrative resources to build malware functionality "on the fly", through resources like PowerShell, Windows Management Instrumentation, and resource kits. For example, there is a security tool called the Windows Credential Editor, or **wce.exe** (https://www.ampliasecurity.com/research/wcefaq.html#whatiswce). This open-source utility was created by an employee of AmpliaSecurity in 2010 (it was not an original part of Microsoft operating system resource kits and it never was a Microsoft utility). The tool allows you to list Windows logon sessions and view, add, change, and delete associated credentials. It is widely used by penetration testers but also by attackers. How do you determine whether the utility is being used for good or evil? That's where context-based detection is needed. Context is covered in Chapter 7.

Chapter 5: Analytic Team Collaboration

The interaction and knowledge sharing within your security operations team are critical components of intrusion analysis, incident response/handling and forensics investigation. Capturing knowledge and learning from each incident is essential to improving your security team's effectiveness. However, this is time-consuming and often isn't done. This chapter discusses challenges to knowledge sharing and describes four resources for capturing workflow and knowledge efficiently.

Analyst Interaction and Capturing Knowledge

Your security operations can capture, store and strategically learn from the way incidents were worked, the thought processes at various points during analysis, the decisions that lead to certain activities, and so on. Unfortunately, too many organizations have deficiencies in capturing this component. Managers and organizational leaders typically see only the result of all that work — perhaps in an incident report or technical report provided to the team. Organizational leaders may see only an executive summary. Maybe it's a "post-incident review" or a collection of the notes entered into a service ticketing system such as Remedy, Service Desk, or ServiceNow.

When football teams aren't practicing, coaches, defensive and offensive advisors and players watch many replays of games. They do it to learn from how the game was executed and to study how their opponents operated during the game.

In the Information/Cyber Security business, most of us are under-resourced, under-staffed and putting out too many fires to collect and store the equivalent of days, weeks or months of work. Typically, knowledge is transferred informally from analyst to analyst. I have seen a few teams promote a written transfer of knowledge, but that's rare. Even rarer are teams where analysts take the time to record the analysis of an event or incident from start to finish.

When ad hoc learning or knowledge transfer like this happens informally, if your analysts shift into other positions or transition out of the team, a great deal of knowledge leaves with them. Analysts who have been on the security operations team for a while will have the institutional background and knowledge to quickly answer questions such as these:

- What is normal endpoint behavior and what is abnormal?
- Who or what group maintains server or cloud provider logs that we need to analyze?

- We need to sweep 50 endpoints across several business units that don't have standard NTP or time synchronization. How do we build a timeline of events when time entries in our logs are not standardized?
- A threat actor is probably active in the network now, but they're on an enclave that doesn't have full packet capture ability. Who is authorized and able to spin up a packet sniffer and what is that process? If the threat actor is monitoring for sniffers or communicating over TLS/SSL, how much will a packet sniffer really see?
- Who is responsible for incident cleanup? The security team is responsible for incident response and handling, but remediation and cleanup may not be their responsibility.
- A contractor heard we had an incident and she wants to report it to her company. What information can be disclosed? From whom? When? To whom?
- I'm not the only one working this incident. Who provides the post-mortem report and when is it required?

When that knowledge is lost, it takes time, effort and resources to rebuild it. That happens again, again and again in many organizations.

In the US Army for decades, troop and combat rotations caused a constant cycle of learning and relearning. The Tactical Internet Ground Reporting System (TIGR) was developed to help alleviate the pains. This system is a great example of what might be required to capture, collect, store and use this type of information within an organization and between elements that rotate in and out. Here is one of many open source resources describing TIGR:

https://gdmissionsystems.com/command-and-control/tactical-ground-reporting-system

Figure 22 shows a publicly released, unclassified screenshot of what the TIGR system looks like:

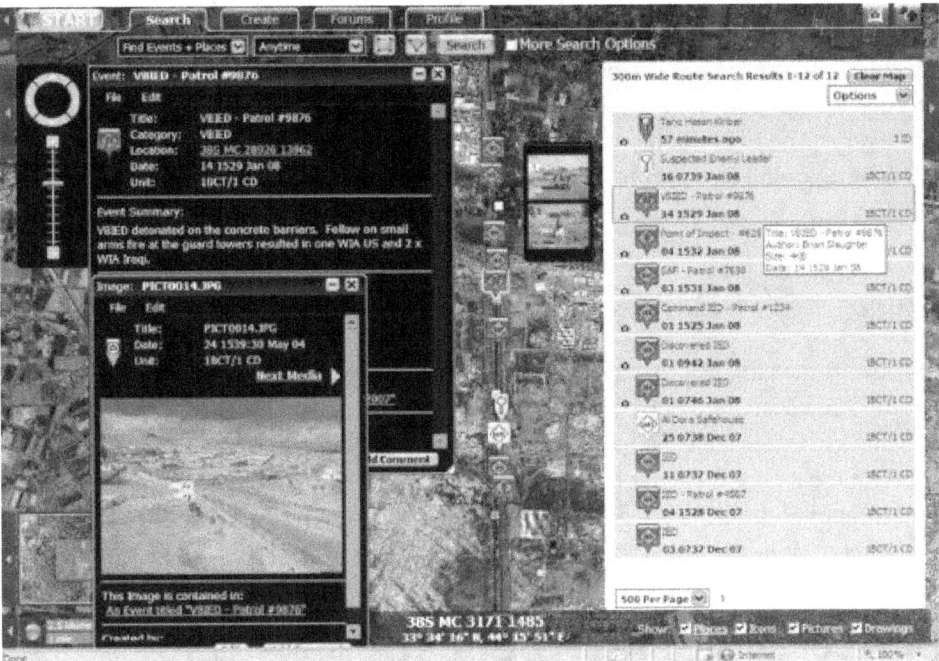

Figure 22: TIGR system

The means of collecting knowledge also matters—for example, capturing annotation or notes in events, recording online chats between analysts, saving photocopies or scanned handwritten notes. You may not think about this until one of the following happens:

- You are asked for information two or three years after an incident because a similar incident happens, or a nation-state threat actor was discovered in your environment and you need to piece together past incidents to form a bigger picture.
- An insider threat case comes up and human resources, legal, counterintelligence, law enforcement or a government agency descends on your security operations team and wants all the past notes, recordings, annotations and details of an incident.

I've been to organizations in the past that have said, "We capture all of that type of communication through email". Bad idea! While email and online storage might be a great central source of knowledge, that is just where most skilled threat actors go first to discover what a security operations team already knows. When 30, 50, 75 or more people or more are included in an incident tracking distribution list, that increases the scope of where sensitive details can be lost. Threat actors may not need to compromise your entire email infrastructure; they only need to compromise one account.

An external military monitoring organization once notified my security team that they had detected our incident details being leaked to a yahoo.com account. We discovered that an army sergeant who handled IS tasks for his unit was going on leave and decided to forward his work email to his AKO us.army.mil account. Unfortunately, when he was on leave, he realized he could not access his AKO account from a non-government computer. He had one of his buddies log in to his AKO account and forward everything to his personal yahoo.com account. Needless to say, there were multiple issues with leaking details to a yahoo.com email address and credential sharing between the sergeant and his buddy.

Capture the Fringe – SOC Shift Changes

Many security operations center teams are shift-oriented. An overlap of 30 minutes to an hour is essential so the two shifts can discuss what is going on, share experiences, highlight incidents and provide continuity. This is also a great time for your team members to share experiences and knowledge not only with the next shift but with everyone on the current shift This often happens in more structured government and military security operations centers but doesn't always happen in commercial organizations or non-military and government groups.

Why IT Service Ticketing Applications Aren't Enough

Many organizations use service ticketing applications. I formerly disliked most of them because they weren't very customizable, they were geared toward the workflow of IT, and digging information out was even harder than putting information in. They were downright useless for some activities of a Tier 2 or 3 analyst or an anomaly detection content creator, such as generating rules, signatures, and conditions. Recently, some applications have been improved using feedback and recommendations from customers. Some have become worse.

Service ticketing and IT management systems are designed primarily to be case tracking tools, not a resource for IS knowledge management and team collaboration. Typically, team leads or managers want to measure how long it takes to close a case. This is easy to measure, and performance is rated based on the ability to close a case. For example, an automatic notification can be sent when a case hasn't been touched in 7 days. However, it's easy for anyone to log in at 6.5 days just to add some comments and reset the timing threshold. This completely defeats the purpose of the trigger.

Case closure time is a terrible measurement from the SECOPS perspective. The real concern is what the issues noted in the ticket were and whether the incident was properly investigated and analyzed. It doesn't matter if it takes two months, six months, or one year. (There is a point at which it is no longer viable to know what the root cause or original issue was. After this point, the value of working an incident decreases as the age of the incident increases.)

Neither a service ticketing system nor ad hoc, analyst-to-analyst transfer of information are optimal for analyst collaboration. But there are other options for capturing knowledge and measurements that support the goals of your security operations team.

FireEye Resources for Capturing Notes and Workflow

Several FireEye products, such as the OpenIOC Editor, Redline, Endpoint Security and Cloud HX, have ways to add tags, comments or notes to events and descriptions for IOCs. Helix incorporates a case management system and the ability to add multiple analyst notes to events.

OpenIOC Editor

When you write an IOC with the OpenIOC Editor, you can add notes or comments either to the entire indicator or to specific conditions of the indicator. The outlined box on the right shows where you can add notes for the entire indicator (Figure 23):

Figure 23: OpenIOC Editor notes

Those cases, categories, caveats, and so on that you add become a searchable part of the OpenIOC application.

You can also add a description for the entire IOC (Figure 24):

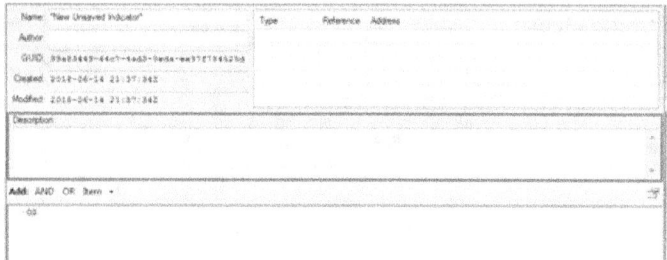

Figure 24: OpenIOC Editor description

I tell students to write descriptions for their IOCs as if they will be read three years from now when the authors are no longer around. The description should be enough to explain the purpose of the IOC and why it contains the components it does, along with any necessary background or context.

You can add notes to individual conditions (Figure 25):

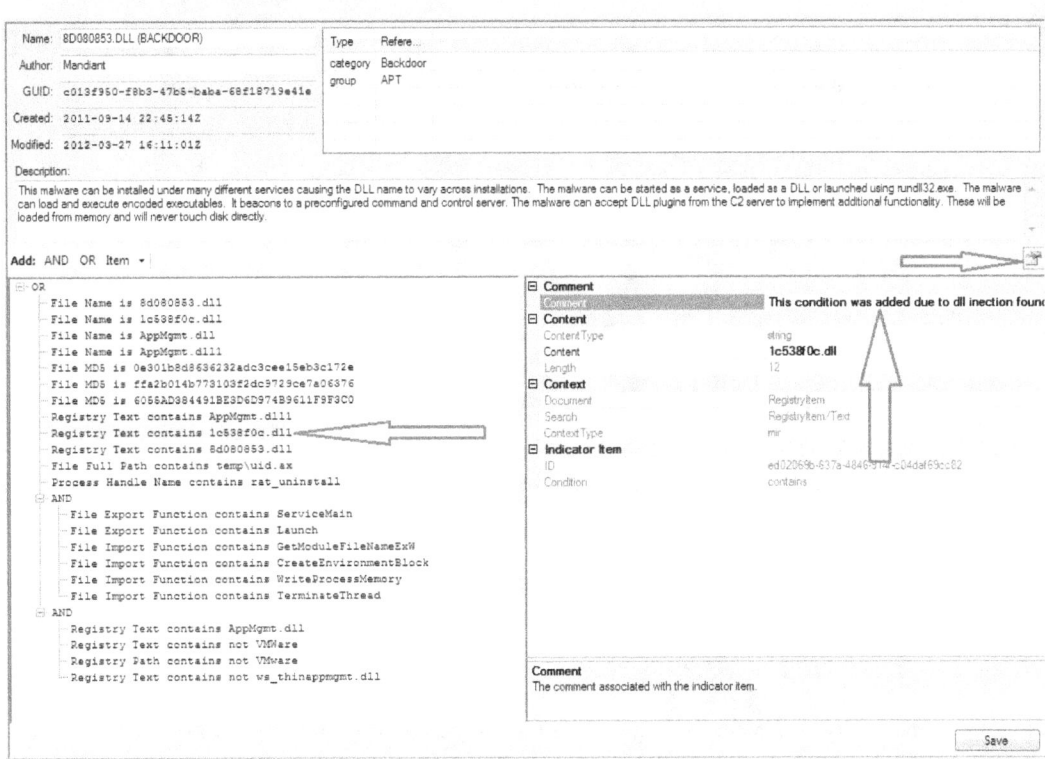

Figure 25: Adding notes

Like comments on IOCs, comments on individual conditions become searchable within the OpenIOC Editor.

The OpenIOC Editor is a stand-alone application and those comments or descriptions are not available externally beyond the application. Since this is a free resource, it doesn't have as many internal development resources available as our commercially available products and platforms. There is no API for the OpenIOC Editor.

Redline

With Redline, you can tag events and add comments to events, as shown in Figure 26:

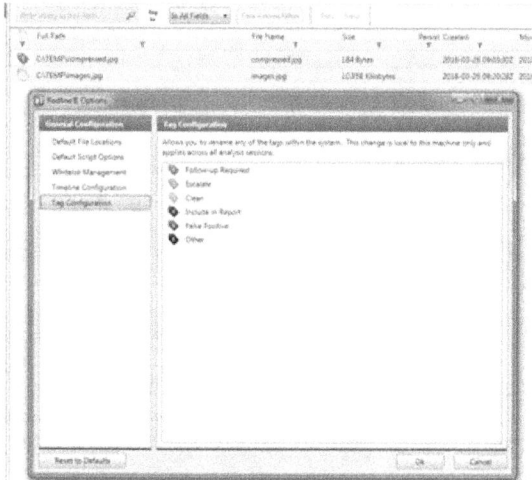

Figure 26: Tagging events in Redline

By clicking the tag icon, you can cycle through six levels of tags, from Follow-up Required to Other. If you don't like the canned names for levels 1-6, you can change them by left-clicking the tag name.

The Full Path section in Figure 27 shows that the file "compressed.jpg" is only 184 bytes — abnormally small for a JPG.

Full Path	File Name	Size
C:\TEMP\compressed.jpg	compressed.jpg	184 Bytes
C:\TEMP\images.jpg	images.jpg	10.858 Kilobytes

Figure 27: Event details in Redline

To add a comment about that, you can click the file name and then click the Tags and Comments tab in the lower-right corner, as seen in Figure 28:

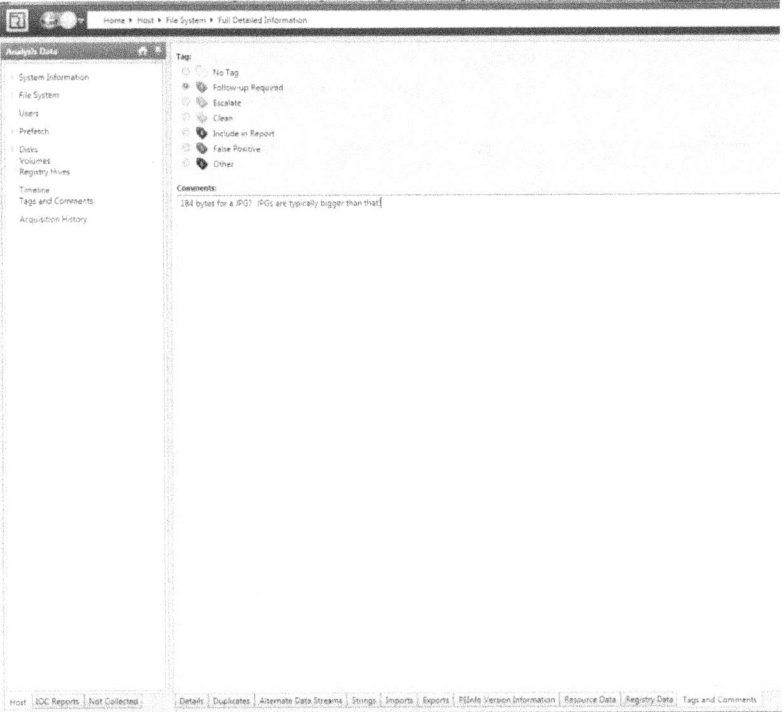

Figure 28: Viewing tags

Clicking the Strings tab reveals something abnormal (Figure 29):

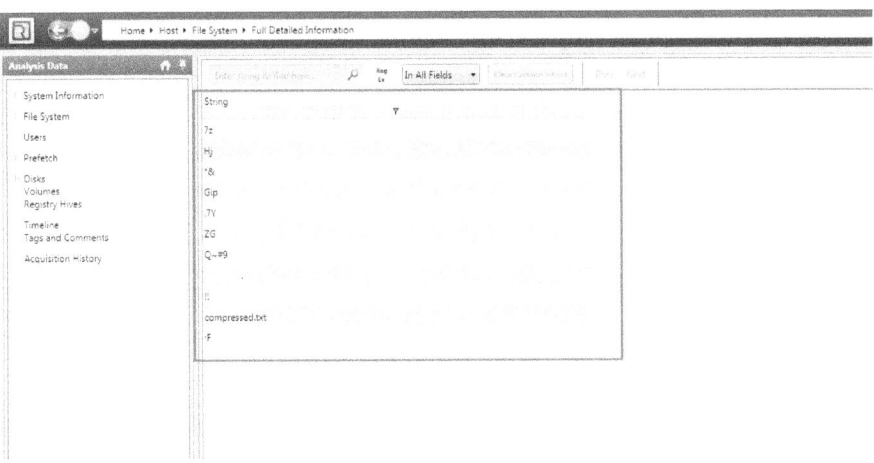

Figure 29: Strings tab

The first string (a reflection of the first entry for the file header) is "7z" and there is a file named "compressed.txt". You might add a comment saying that maybe this file isn't really a JPG.

In Redline, you can display all the tags and comments by clicking on the Tags and Comments section of the Analysis Data pane on the left side of the application (Figure 30).

Figure 30: Viewing all tags and comments

As with the OpenIOC Editor, when you add comments or tags on objects in Redline, they become searchable within Redline.

Redline is a stand-alone application and those comments and tags are not available outside the application. Since Redline is a free resource that doesn't have as many internal development resources available as we have for our commercially available products and platforms, future expansion of functions and capabilities will be limited.

FireEye Endpoint Security Server (HX)

The FireEye Endpoint Security server (HX Series) has two areas for comments and descriptions. When you write an indicator (called a *rule* in 4.5.x and later), there is a description field (Figure 31):

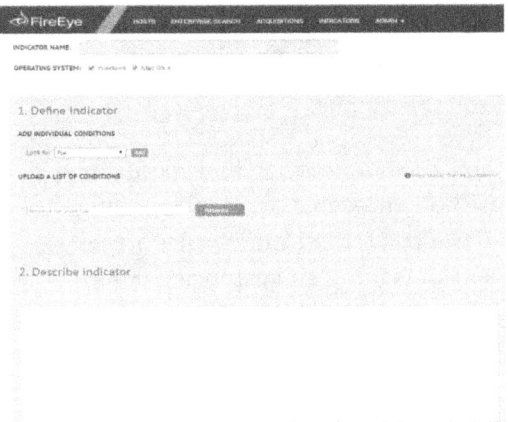

Figure 31: HX indicator description field

In the HX Audit Viewer, when you open the details of an event, you can tag events and add comments (Figure 32):

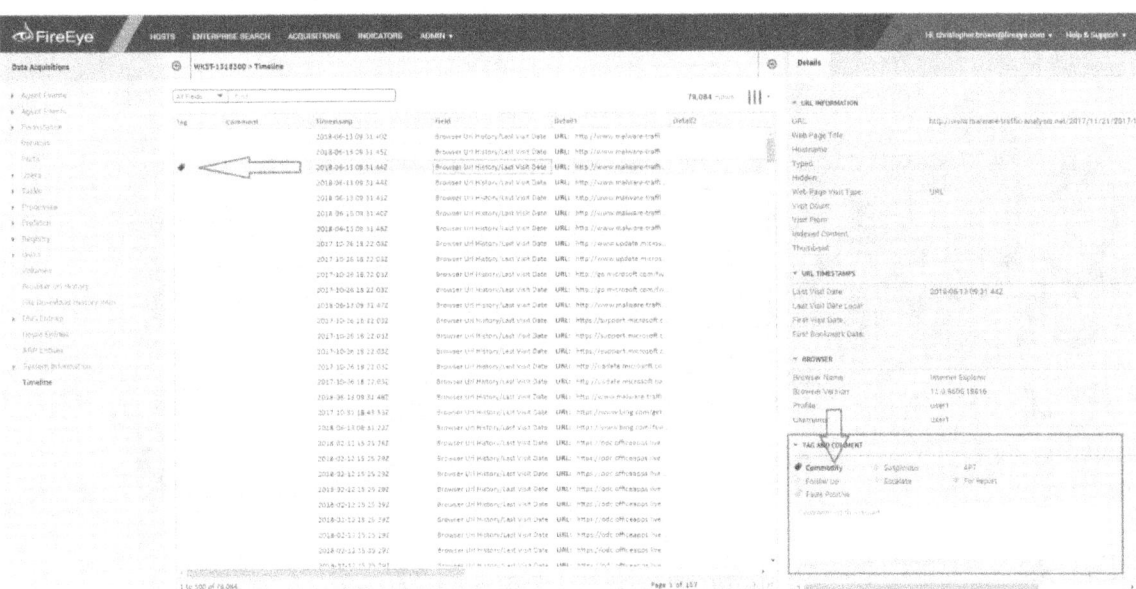

Figure 32: HX Audit Viewer

Your tags and comments become searchable within that host's audit viewer. You can also search for indicators/rules by name, author, signature name or conditional value. You can also add a description to indicators of compromise.

I know it takes more time to document descriptions and metadata like this. A description that answers the question, "Why does this IOC exist and what was the analyst thinking?" is way more effective than "Created IOC based on service ticket 745292".

Notes and tags in the audit viewer are available only within the audit view on that specific controller. As of this writing, comments and event tags are not retrievable or writable through the HX API. You cannot search based on description and descriptions for indicators/rules are not forwarded to Helix. However, in Helix, there is a better way of tagging and capturing descriptions and comments across a team level.

Helix

Of all FireEye products and platforms, Helix has the most to offer for workflow, collaboration, a case management system, and searching notes made by analysts or members of your security operations team that have access to the Helix console. Figure 33 shows a Cloud HX alert in Helix 1.3.

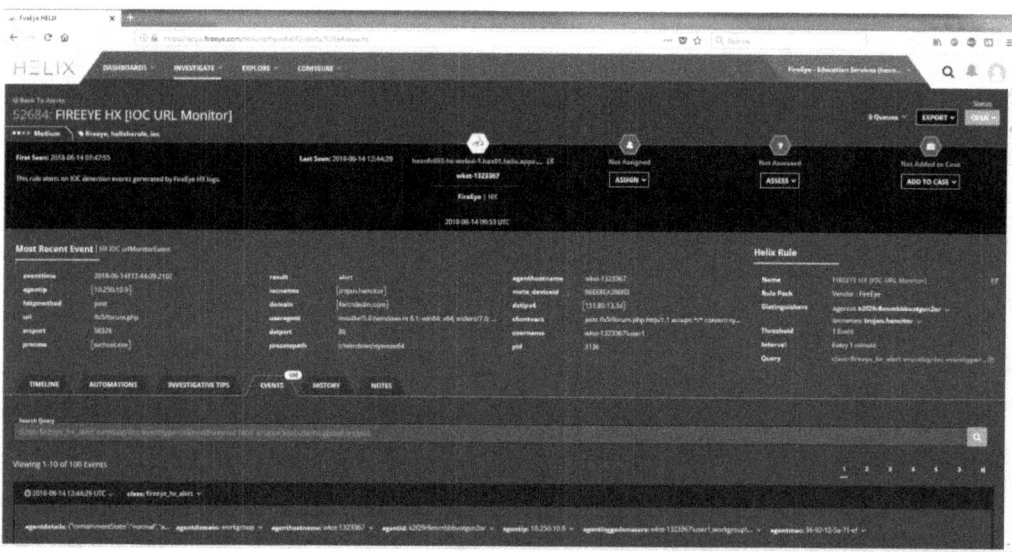

Figure 33: Helix alert

You can add notes on the NOTES tab or view an entire case (Figure 34):

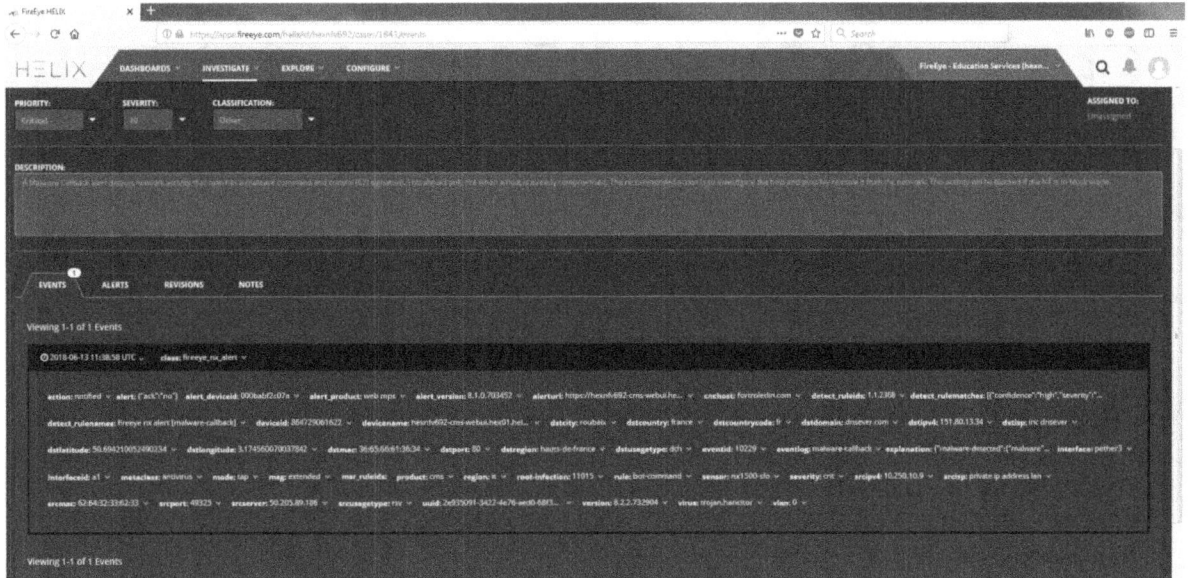

Figure 34: Helix case

Helix, as a platform, is extensible and has the foundations to build in almost any capability.

Chapter 6: Analyst Fatigue and Analytic Biases

The first three chapters of the book provided key concepts for security operations best practices. Now we will highlight topics that often become pain points at various levels. Some of these pain points can be more acute than others but each contributes to overall suffering that can expand across an entire security team or security operations center.

This chapter addresses challenges to human factors that can hinder security operations. These are driven by the avalanche of information our security teams must deal with daily, technology gaps that require an analyst to jump between various resources (sometimes multiple resources from the same vendor or manufacturer), and translating terminology because what one vendor calls an event, another vendor calls an alert, and a third vendor calls an alarm. I'll discuss five major challenges and then offer recommendations for overcoming them.

The major challenges are:

- Alert saturation
- Event fatigue
- Attention erosion
- Analytic biases
- Analyst paralysis

Pushing the boundaries beyond the resources most of us have, over the long term, will lead to negative results. Analysts burn out, attrition increases, quality of professional life deteriorates.

Alert saturation and event fatigue are familiar to every analyst. Attention erosion can be more insidious. In a former environment I won't name, some of the smarter members of the team were worn down by the extremely noisy surroundings. They started their shifts by logging in and spinning up resources like their IDS event collectors, logging appliances and a SIEM, and then let the events roll past them like waves washing over a beach. They played music through their headsets and somewhat zoned out until they saw a high-priority event cross their screen. If they caught one or two a day, great. If not, the team was large enough that they hoped someone else would catch the others. This detachment was their only way to protect themselves, but the effects on security are obvious.

The current trend of open offices to facilitate collaboration and sharing has major drawbacks for a cyber security team. Some organizations think it's OK to throw their information security team together in a space that resembles a beehive or telemarketing operation, with 50, 75, 100 or more desks in rows. While it's important for teams to collaborate and share, information and security analysis—incident response/handling, forensics work, writing anomaly/malicious detection content like correlation rules and conditions—require critical thinking and attention to detail. These are not facilitated by a noisy, distracting environment. A security operations team also deals with some very sensitive issues, such as user credentials, intellectual property being collected or captured through malware, potential insider threat activity (whether intentional or not), and potential legal and counterintelligence issues. There is no privacy or confidentiality in a call center environment.

The last topic in this chapter is analytic biases. We all have them in one form or another, and we can learn to recognize them over time. We must fight against those biases constantly. In this business, many of us are counted on to be experts who base their observations, assessments and recommendations on facts. When those facts are missing or are hazy at best, our biases might creep in as a substitute. As stated in Chapter 2, "It doesn't matter what I believe; it only matters what I can prove". Everything else is subjective. When we make observations, assessments or recommendations based on things we can't validate or can't prove, that can lead to a bias. Gut feelings and personal intuition have a place, especially in hunting to develop an initial hypothesis. But it's essential to be aware of the difference and to know when you are using facts or gut feelings.

One of my favorite lines from the movie Crimson Tide is, "We have rules that are not open to interpretation, personal intuition, gut feelings, hairs on the back of our neck, little devils or angels sitting on our shoulders". I advise being careful with interpretation (especially without the right context or background) and relying more on what we can prove through logs telemetry and measurements than on intuition.

Alert Saturation

Alert saturation is when you simply have too many alerts and not enough analysts. Objects being analyzed are usually in four states:

- Objects that are currently being analyzed or run through active engines
- Objects that are waiting in a queue and haven't been analyzed yet
- Objects that have been dropped and will never make it into the queue or through active detection engines
- Objects that have been analyzed and are held for blocking and quarantine or delivered to an endpoint for later analysis

Analysts and security operations centers and teams all have their limits. When those limits are reached, you're saturated. Your buckets are full.

A targeted threat actor can exploit this state using a technique is known as "smoke screening". The attacker or threat actor deliberately creates conditions that generate enough alerts and events to flood an IDS console or SIEM client or logging device. Hundreds or thousands of events will flood into the security operations center. The attacker counts on the fact that your team will not be able to handle them all or will be too distracted or saturated to focus on other areas.

A popular method for a smokescreen attack is to mount a DDoS (distributed denial of service) attack that trips bandwidth alarms, causing latency thresholds, congestion concerns, loss of availability and, of course, causing services to lock up or stop responding. When the threat actor is already in your network and wants to engage in malicious activity that would probably be detected and analyzed on a normal day, they'll generate a DDoS as a smokescreen and then quietly work their malicious activity during the same time.

You don't even need a malicious threat actor to cause alert saturation. We do that on our own by generating too many alerts from a multitude of sensor grids, detection devices, point products and endpoint security resources.

Event Fatigue

This is a variation of alert saturation. Too many events degrade an analyst or security team's ability to work events to their completion. Essentially, it's a condition of being too tired or fatigued to continue. It's a challenge just to step back and recognize this condition. It can affect an individual analyst or it can escalate to the entire team.

In combat operations, this is known as "the fight is wearing us down". This is also a technique used in Advanced Persistent Threats by an intrusion-problem set threat actor or a focused operator. They are counting on your team to reach a level where they just can't continue to work events because they are mentally exhausted.

Event fatigue, if it goes on long enough, contributes toward attrition and loss of team members. It dulls a security team's edge. Individual analysts may start missing details and clues to bad behavior—even something as simple as noticing the difference between the words ADMIN and ADMN in a log file.

The term *inattentional blindness* is often applied to other analytic professions. This is when we, as humans, lose the ability to focus our attention on something that requires critical thinking or skill. We all have limited attention spans and can generally only focus on a limited number of things at a time.

Our business—especially at the security operations center and team level—involves gazing into multiple screens looking for anomalies or digging through hundreds of thousands of lines of logs or events. If you ever want to throw someone into immediate event fatigue just so they can get an idea of what most of us go through, sit them down at an inline connected network detection device, spin up a console and run tcpdump -vv. Then count the seconds until their eyes glaze over.

Attention Erosion

One of my favorite ThinkGeek t-shirts only has 3.5 words on it:

I never finish anyth

Attention erosion is a real issue. A recent book on the subject is titled "Distracted: The Erosion of Attention and the Coming Dark Age" https://www.amazon.com/dp/B003A842VW/ref=dp-kindle-redirect?_encoding=UTF8&btkr=1)

Every time I hear someone say, "we must do more with less," I cringe. Often, the person saying that is not the one who must deal with the results. There is a litany of repercussions when we attempt to do more with less. Busy professional lives, too much work, not enough time and inadequate resources contribute to fragmented focus and attempts to multitask beyond what we can reasonably handle—factors that negatively impact the business of information security.

As a ham radio operator in my teens, I volunteered on weekends as a network controller for the Maritime Mobile Service Network. I enjoyed the fast pace of controlling or linking up hundreds of connections between radio operators looking for everything from weather reports, to updates on news and sports scores, to radio phone patches. My dad suggested that I consider a career as an air traffic controller. I scored well on the exam after studying for a few weeks and got on a few hiring rosters. But reality sank in after I toured a few control towers and watched terminal controllers handle massive amounts of incoming and outgoing aircraft during what controllers called "crunch time". Air traffic controllers must be prepared to handle their sectors whether their radar scope is operational or not (it might scare you to know how often radar scopes went down in the 1980s). They must conceptually keep track of air traffic, through 3-dimensional airspace, with nothing but a radio. It was a level of attention that I knew I couldn't handle. This is also why the FAA requires most controllers to retire from active "scope duty" when they reach their mid-40s. Air traffic controllers cannot lose their ability to focus—in their business, attention erosion risks life and limb.

In information security, death and injury aren't typically a consequence of attention erosion. However, the consequences are serious enough. When incidents impact an entire organization, customers no longer trust it with their money, personal information, or long-term loyalty.

The introduction to this chapter described ways a distracting environment can hinder critical thinking and erode your ability to focus and stay attentive for long periods of time. Knowing our personal preferences and limits is also important. In my 20s, I could write intrusion detection signatures or filters and take certification tests at almost any time of day. Now that I'm older, I'm best at detail-oriented activities like writing scripts in the early morning. I never take a certification exam after noon. Other people may hit their peak in the afternoon. We all know what our best conditions and our limits are. We need to plan for them during security operations execution—and to be aware that they can change over time.

We also need the self-awareness to recognize when we are losing focus or becoming distracted.

Analytic Biases

Analytic biases affect, at some level, anyone who has worked an analyst desk, engaged in incident response/handling or dug through forensic images and analyzed the data. They especially affect those who know enough to be dangerous but haven't gained enough field experience to realize that things aren't always what they seem be. When hackers and threat actors are doing anything they can to evade detection, skating around deployed defensive and protection resources, it's important to remember a saying (applicable equally to our profession and to professional wrestling):

"Believe half of what you hear and none of what you see."

We fill the gap between appearance and reality with ideas that may well spring from our biases. I've got mine built up through decades of background, experiences and knowledge.

The American astrophysicist and author Neil deGrasse Tyson has often discussed the following example of bias. When an unknown object is in the sky, there are many that will say "It has got to be alien". By definition, a UFO is an "unidentified flying object". Therefore, it is unknown. The assumption that it must be alien is a perfect example of bias. Old-timers in IS and IT remember the saying, "You'll never go wrong with IBM"; investors remember, "You can't be criticized for buying IBM stock." The perception expressed in these sayings is a vendor/manufacturer bias.

In cyber security, all of us learn the basics of ports, protocols and services quickly. We learn that SMTP runs on port 25, DNS on port 53, and HTTP on port 80. And we would have absorbed a bias. Those services are commonly associated with those ports, but nothing *requires* those protocols to be bound to those ports. There have been SSL interception products that failed to parse HTTP unencrypted network traffic that ran over port 443—because they were designed to expect HTTP unencrypted traffic only on the traditional port 80.

In other types of analysis, such as military intelligence and counterintelligence, biases are often discussed. The academic community has many studies and papers published on analytic bias, often under the name *cognitive bias.*

We cover common biases that can negatively impact your security operations team below, but this is not an all-encompassing list. You'll probably be able to add to these categories and if you can, I'd love to know.

Malware of the Week Bias

Also known as an *availability heuristic,* this is a mental shortcut that relies on examples that come to mind immediately when we evaluate a particular topic, concept, method or decision. The availability heuristic operates on the notion that if something can be recalled, it must be important. Malware involved with the most recent intrusions and compromises, whatever it was, will come to mind first.

Confirmation Bias

We tend to interpret new information to confirm our current views, and to discount data that contradicts or presents an alternative to our views. This often happens in information security when there is a belief that certain defensive, detection and protection resources work the best. By amplifying the successes and ignoring or discounting their shortcomings, we inflate their overall effectiveness.

Information Bias

This one is easily described: more alerts or events are always better, without regard to their value, efficacy, weighting or gravity. In information security, more is not better. On the contrary, more information can often lead to less value per alert or event, and to weaker decisions because there is too much noise compared to actual signal.

Popularity Bias

This is like the malware of the week bias. Buzzwords and hot topics become the rage with little or no substance behind them. At any of the big cyber security conferences, especially if you trend the discussions and hot topics over years, you'll see the popularity bias in action. One year, all the vendors are talking about "Big Data Analytics." The next year, it might be "Governance, Risk and Compliance," and the following year it might be "Artificial Intelligence". All these topics are important, but no single one is a complete solution.

Over-Reliance on Security Technology Bias

Those of us who travel for work know the risk of espionage or counterintelligence. We encrypt the hard drives on our laptops to keep them safe in case we're asked during an airport security screening to open and turn them on. Unfortunately, over-reliance on encryption can turn out very negatively if we don't consider all the variables that could alter or disrupt the decryption process. Consider the following scenario:

- You are asked to open your laptop, power it up and log in during a security screening. The security officer then asks you to log off while they insert a USB drive to scan your system for illegal content that is not allowed in the country. You're confident that a scan will find nothing untoward, because your information is encrypted. However, you don't know the context or the real purpose of that USB drive. Unknown to you (and perhaps to the security staff as well), that USB drive might be scraping or capturing your laptop's physical memory.
- As required, you also disclose the address of your hotel on the customs and immigrations form.
- The next evening, after your first day at work, you log off your laptop and leave it closed and powered on while you go to dinner with colleagues. A "special staff member" enters your room with your local username and password, obtained from the memory capture that was run from the USB "scanning device" in the airport. The staff member proceeds to log in to your system. Game over.

Distrusting Your Instrumentation Bias

All biases are bad, but this is one of the most dangerous. At FireEye, we get a moderate number of service tickets and customer success issues created for alerts that customers perceive to be false positives. When we run those to ground or perform root cause analysis, a surprising number are not false positives – they were legitimate true positive events.

Distrusting your instrumentation is like attempting to fly visually when the conditions require instrument flying rules—it creates a very dangerous situation. It is believed that the death of John F. Kennedy Jr. occurred because he was piloting a private plane in weather that required instrument flying, which he was not rated for. Though he was only rated for visual flight rules, he took his chances and flew anyway—a fatal mistake.

Analyst Paralysis

In a DDoS attack, so many packets and so much traffic is directed at a port, service, daemon or resource that the resource stops functioning. Port availability can be exhausted, services or daemons can shut down, resources can effectively be killed or terminated. Analyst paralysis happens when analysts are overwhelmed by the sheer volume and velocity of alerts, alarms, events, and information that flood their eyes and ears. As in the biologic response of "fight, flight, or freeze," the analysts shut down or disengage from the mission.

Recommendations to Reduce Alert Saturation

It's easy to think alert saturation is unavoidable. If you cut down the number of alerts to align with your resources, you risk missing something critical. Here are five recommendations that can ease the pain of alert saturation.

- **Tune your signatures.** Whether they're IDS signatures, A/V definitions, proxy filters applied to a log—most filters, signatures, definitions, and correlated rules have a mechanism to throttle the number of alerts generated based on aggregation settings. Let's take the Snort rule from an earlier chapter:

  ```
  alert tcp $EXTERNAL_NET any -> $SQL_SERVERS 1443 (msg:"SQL brute force
  login attempt"; flow:to_server,established; content:"|02|"; depth:1;
  offset:39; nocase; detection_filter; track by_src, count 5, seconds 30;
  reference:redacted; classtype:suspicious-loging; sid:99999;rev:8)
  ```

  Notice track by_src, count 5, seconds 30. Instead of logging the first 5 events every 30 seconds, maybe we only need to count 5 events every two minutes. Adjusting the aggregation settings on your signatures helps reduce the number of alerts generated.

- **Augment your staff.** If you don't want (or can't afford) to increase your staff long term, consider bringing in a team as surge support. FireEye offers a service that supports the requirements you will have regarding staff augmentation. Formerly called FaaS or FireEye as a Service, this service is now called MD or Managed Defense.

- **Consider automation.** Since it's the machines that are generating more alerts than we humans can keep up with, we can use the recent improvements made in automation and orchestration to let machines take some of the load and stress off our analysts. We'll cover automation and orchestration in a later chapter.

- **Consider SECOPS.** By integrating security operations at a machine level or fusing together some IT resources with your IS resources, you'll be able to prune some of the events or alerts that might be noise or false positives.

- **Talk to your analysts.** See what they recommend. The teams I have worked with and supported as a lead have always had ideas about how we can help make their professional lives easier and better. One analyst that I worked with observed that while day shift seemed to be saturated with alerts, the volume and velocity of alerts during evening shift wasn't as bad. Nothing says that your night shift or swing shift analysts can look only at events generated on their shift. Almost every team has slow times when they can share the load from time to time.

Recommendations to Combat Event Fatigue

Sometimes event fatigue is temporary; other times it is long-term. Many of the recommendations for dealing with alert saturation can also apply to event fatigue. Here are additional recommendations.

- **Actively pursue peer review.** If an analyst or security team member has been working for days on an incident, looping in another resource to take over for a while will not only help with event fatigue; it also brings in a new set of eyes. Every analyst, especially when suffering from fatigue or inattentional blindness, has unique blind spots. Even when I thought I wasn't tired, when I thought I was near the end of an incident or set of events that I was working, I would ask one or two of my colleagues to spot-check my work. This technique is especially practical for your junior or newer team members who may not have the background or perspective that experienced team members can bring to the table, but it helps seasoned analysts, too.

- **Use resources or tools that help you annotate and tag events.** I love tshark for scripting analysis of packets. WireShark uses colors in the GUI to highlight certain conditions or states, making them much easier to see. Sysinternals resources like Process Monitor and Process Explorer (described in Chapter 2) use colors as well.

- **Use graphics to visualize security events.** I'm a firm believer in security event visualization. In this business, one picture is worth a thousand log lines. Create heat maps, density maps (for example, the number of events per IDS sensor), or something else that can dynamically, in real time, display rapidly changing security conditions across your entire network. I'm not talking about basic bar charts or pie graphs that serve as eye candy for visitors, but about visualization on security operations monitors that are designed for the analyst. One open-source tool for creating effective visualization for security events is SecViz (https://www.secviz.org/).

- **Distinguish event fatigue from lack of knowledge or skill.** Qualified security operations professionals—analysts, incident responders and handlers, content writers—not only understand your tools and resources but also have foundational knowledge of networks and how different operating systems and applications process data. They are engaged, driven and always asking questions. A person who often seems drained or disengaged may simply lack the skills to drive an incident or the experience to ask the right questions. Make sure your current or potential team members aren't in over their heads.

Recommendations for Dealing with Attention Erosion

- **Use resources that allow you to work with blocks of information or data you can consume at one time.** It isn't effective to try and analyze a block of data that contains 875,000 events or a log of 1.2 million lines. I recommend you begin with a pivot point. Go to where you know you should start, then expand your field from there. FireEye products provide many ways to do that Let's say you use Redline during a live response incident to run a standard or comprehensive collector, only to find you've collected 853,517 events. You can use filtering, TimeWrinkles, or TimeCrunches to pivot through that wide range of events, or you can configure the collector to be more selective.

- **Ask your team.** Ask your analysts, incident responders/handlers, and security operations team members what detracts from their ability to maintain optimal attention to detail or obtain the critical thinking environment they require.

- **Look for specific signs:**

    o Sudden variances in work output.
    o Engagement levels seem to drop without explanation.
    o Side projects are started but don't seem to get finished.
    o When you ask for status updates, answers are vague or don't reflect acceptable progress.
    o Long hours at work with little output to show for them.
    o Casual conversations about what your colleagues or direct reports plan for their shift result in "I don't know" or "I'll find something to do". Both are typical ways of saying, "I have no plans."

- **Protect your team.** Do this whether you are a colleague looking out for other colleagues or a supervisor, team lead or security operations manager.

○ Each new resource for detection, defense or protection typically requires a minimum of three to five more analysts (unless there are mitigating factors, such as an automation or integration solution). If you run two 12-hour shifts, you need at least one analyst for each shift and one as a backup. You need five if you are shooting for 24x7x365 coverage, to accommodate vacations, leaves or special projects. Don't forget to plan for one or more administrators, depending on the size and scale of the new resource.

○ Keep tabs on the event/alert/alarm flow through your security operations center. Sustained or persistent high levels can overwhelm a team. When I was an operations lead of analyst teams, my higher-ups expected me to know our daily (sometimes hourly) events per second was and the reasons for any significant change.

Recommendations for Managing Analytic Biases

This is a tough one. However, I have a few recommendations:

- **Keep asking questions to validate your theories.** Biases can creep in due to lack of scientific proof or lack of context or additional correlation. If I see a string of alerts titled "Attempted DNS Amplification Attack in Progress" from my IDS, I want to know exactly what sensors those alerts came from. Especially if we have no IDS sensors in our DMZ or on the north (Internet-facing) side of our firewalls. A DNS amplification attack coming from an internal resource is not completely impossible, but my first effort is to gauge the efficacy of those alerts.

- **Get different points of view.** If you have the resources, spread the analysis of a specific incident, intrusion, breach or compromise among at least two or three analysts. Everyone has a unique background, diverse experience and specific history or organizational knowledge to bring to your security team. Have your team engage in peer reviews or analyst colleague reviews.

- **Don't be afraid to play devil's advocate.** Some of my best intrusion analysis work was done when I could bounce ideas off someone else. Remember, not everything will be as it first appears.

- **Promote team collaboration.** Enable the capture and replay of that collaboration so others can learn.

- **Trust your data.** Decisions made primarily on hunches, gut feelings or intuition can lead to biases of various types. Don't disregard the instrumentation. If you think an incident is moving in a certain direction, trust the data. In the absence of data, do all you can to caveat your thoughts. Be cautious about making an assessment when you lack data to validate your theories.

Recommendations for Preventing Analyst Paralysis

- **Get your team away from the glass.** Get them away from their monitors and into an environment where they feel comfortable at giving candid and honest feedback without the fear of being marginalized or criticized. Hear them out. Ask them what leads to analyst paralysis and their recommendations for adding mitigation or some method of compensating control before the paralysis state is reached.

- **Use the resources you already have.** Filtering, aggregation of alerts, deploying better correlated rules to start piecing together conditions related to multiple events for a bigger picture, and reduction in event and alert noise can all help. If your organization faces extreme conditions, consider bringing in security orchestration and automation.

- **Identify contributing factors.** We all know and love the OSI 7-layer model. Look for unofficial "layers" that contribute to analyst paralysis. Layer 8 may be a people problem. Layer 9 could be an organizational issue. Layer 10 might be issues with auditing, government or legal compliance. Your organization may have its own unique "layers" or points of friction.

Chapter 7: Why Context Is King

Context can be defined as the circumstances that form the setting for an event, statement, or idea, and in terms of which it can be fully understood and assessed. You can ask almost any cyber security analyst or security operations team member, "What can you never have enough of?" Along with monitors, storage space and RAM, one of their top answers will be *context*. Almost every security operations team and information security group I've ever worked with or trained has a long-term deficiency in context.

While many IS vendors still specialize in certain areas, the vendors that provide platform-level functionality and resources or capabilities that fill the gaps in context are the ones that will endure the next decade of maturation that I strongly feel our industry requires. For many security organizations, no one resource currently provides enough context, functionality or situational knowledge to make an informed decision. Years of adding "one more resource" to the mix of tools results in a spaghetti-tangled mess of alarms, alerts, events, packet captures, detection grids, protection systems, IDS resources, enterprise security managers, big data analytics products, custom tools, and so on.

The security operations profession requires vast amounts of data, at the right time, in the right format, in the right context to make informed decisions that require critical thinking and skills. Yet day in and day out, we must deal with lack of information and fragmented efforts, and jump between multiple resources to piece together a bigger picture. We may need to make guesses based on imperfect data; we may have to caveat our decisions with "There is insufficient data available to make an accurate analysis". If surgeons had to do their jobs the way we do hours, they'd constantly be stopping to hunt for tools or medical records while the patient is on the operating table.

Why Context Is Hard to Acquire

To provide more context, we buy whatever is needed and deploy it as soon as possible. When that new, shiny, highly praised resource arrives, we find out that while some questions can now be answered, more pop up. Or what we saw in pre-sales and the proof-of-concept phase looked great, but when the product is deployed, it doesn't work as smoothly as in the demo. Figure 35 is an example from a popular SIEM. This problem is not unique to the vendor—all SIEMs have the same issue:

End Time	Name	Source Address	RF Source Context.URL	Source User Name	Target Address
5/13 3:42:32	New Unencrypted Service running on 10.2.195.80				10.2.195.80
5/13 3:42:32	Unencrypted SMTP Traffic Detected	192.156.61.5			10.2.195.80
5/13 3:42:18	Successful Configuration Change				0.0.0.0
5/13 3:41:05	Connector Down				
5/13 3:40:48	New Unencrypted Service running on 10.0.234.237				
5/13 3:40:48	Unencrypted SMTP Traffic Detected	192.156.61.5			10.0.234.237
5/13 3:40:23	New Unencrypted Service running on 192.168.20.8				192.168.20.8
5/13 3:40:23	Unencrypted netbios-ns Traffic Detected	24.86.160.562			
5/13 3:40:08	Hostile - Attempt	66.45.113.197			
5/13 3:39:41	Compromise - Attempt	192.168.20.70			239.255.255.250
5/13 3:39:04	Unencrypted telnet Traffic Detected	134.154.86.215			204.102.253.2
5/13 3:39:04	Compromise - Attempt	134.154.86.215			204.102.253.2
5/13 3:39:01	Probable Successful Attack - Repetitive Exploit Events				192.168.10.134
5/13 3:38:49	Unencrypted SMTP Traffic Detected	10.0.234.237			192.156.61.5
5/13 3:38:46	Hostile - Attempt	6.6.6.6			3.3.3.3
5/13 3:38:33	New Unencrypted Service running on 192.168.20.5				192.168.20.5
5/13 3:38:33	Unencrypted netbios-ns Traffic Detected	200.76.193.34			192.168.20.5
5/13 3:38:32	Successful Configuration Change				0.0.0.0
5/13 3:37:50	New Unencrypted Service running on 216.82.255.35				216.82.255.35
5/13 3:37:43	New Unencrypted Service running on 192.168.20.5				192.168.20.5
5/13 3:37:43	Unencrypted netbios-ns Traffic Detected	200.76.193.34			192.168.20.5
5/13 3:37:40	Connector Down				
5/13 3:37:34	Hostile - Attempt	6.6.6.6			2.2.2.2
5/13 3:37:28	Unencrypted telnet Traffic Detected	134.154.86.13			204.102.253.2
5/13 3:37:28	Compromise - Attempt	134.154.86.13			204.102.253.2
5/13 3:37:25	Unencrypted telnet Traffic Detected	134.154.2.223			204.102.253.2
5/13 3:37:25	Compromise - Attempt	134.154.2.223			204.102.253.2
5/13 3:37:22	Unencrypted telnet Traffic Detected	134.154.15.131			204.102.253.2
5/13 3:37:22	Compromise - Attempt	134.154.15.131			204.102.253.2
5/13 3:37:16	Hostile - Attempt	6.6.6.6			1.1.1.1
5/13 3:36:40	Hostile - Attempt	130.177.241.6			192.85.50.83
5/13 3:36:09	Hostile - Attempt	5.5.5.5			3.3.3.3
5/13 3:36:06	Hostile - Attempt	6.6.6.6			2.2.2.2
5/13 3:36:04	Connector Down				
5/13 3:36:02	Compromise - Attempt				208.249.124.247
5/13 3:35:58	Unencrypted telnet Traffic Detected	134.154.86.24			204.102.253.2
5/13 3:35:58	Compromise - Attempt	134.154.86.24			204.102.253.2
5/13 3:35:54	New Unencrypted Service running on 192.168.10.0				192.168.10.0
5/13 3:35:54	Unencrypted netbios-ns Traffic Detected	192.168.10.132			192.168.10.0
5/13 3:35:53	Hostile - Attempt	5.5.5.5			1.1.1.1
5/13 3:35:44	Successful Configuration Change				0.0.0.0
5/13 3:35:21	Hostile - Attempt	148.94.0.134			192.85.47.87
5/13 3:35:02	Hostile - Attempt	66.179.14.113			
5/13 3:34:54	New Unencrypted Service running on 192.168.20.9				192.168.20.9
5/13 3:34:54	Unencrypted snmp Traffic Detected	192.168.20.72			192.168.20.9
5/13 3:34:46	Hostile - Attempt	4.4.4.4			3.3.3.3

Figure 35: Missing context in a SIEM

Note the gaps where there are big ovals. The two biggest gaps are in the following fields:

- RF Source Context URL (which appears to be a custom field based on the acronym RF)
- Source User Name

Two other fields have gaps in some events:

- Source Address
- Target Address

One of the most common reasons for gaps is that the source of the event didn't have the right type of data to populate all the fields. Another common reason is that the data was there but the parser or tokenizer that handles the data from the collector (or agent) couldn't do its job, so the data didn't make it through the SIEM's database to the user interface on the console. Parsers are responsible for taking input data and extracting the data to create a structure. Tokenizers are responsible for taking that data and creating tokens that are massaged, normalized or transferred into a universal format that the SIEM can use.

This is a notable example of where context is needed. A member of your security operations team using the SIEM must now make a judgement call. Is it OK to continue analyzing events that lack source user name, context URL, source addresses or target addresses? If not, where does the analyst get that information?

Another example: Did you notice multiple lines in the figure above that read "connector down" (Figure 36)?

| 5/13 3:37:40 | Connector Down | | | |

Figure 36: Missing context

As an analyst, my first questions would be *which* connector went down, and for how long. The answers may be available to a SIEM administrator or connector/agent admin, and they're definitely available somewhere—possibly on a heads-up display or dashboard that uses red, yellow, and green icons to represent event flows per connector. But they are not contained in the event and not visible to the analyst.

Recall our example from Chapter 3 and SECOPS. An analyst is required to make split-second decisions several times per minute. It could take an entire minute to figure out where to obtain the missing information. An analyst now must shift gears, stop thinking like an analyst and start thinking like a SIEM Administrator in order to get more details—*context*—about the connector failure, and about what events or alerts are no longer visible as a result.

The missing data for the columns of source user name and source address might have been visible when you previewed the product during the sales cycle. The data in the preview is typically being replayed into the product. Like listening to a recording or watching a video, you're looking at previously captured packets, events or data, not a live feed. A critical question to ask any vendor when you're considering their product is, "What data am I looking at?".

The next question that should pop up is, "Where will I get the live data to populate those fields and how consistent is the data flow to keep those fields populated all the time?". You just hit on the nerve of *context*.

Alert Severity, Event Priority, and the Gravity of Weightings

Almost every resource deployed in support of a security operations team that generates alerts, events, and alarms has something to indicate the importance of an event. There is no standardization of these across vendors and most vendors have different names for these levels of importance, including:

- Severity
- Criticality
- Priority
- Ranking
- Category
- Classification

Too many customers rely on the vendor's terminology (whatever it may be) to assign weighting or judge the importance of an event. When I teach, I often show the students a console displaying multiple events of various levels of importance and ask, "How would you triage these events?" It's rare to get a consensus, but invariably some students say, "Go after the events that have the highest priority/severity/category."

What you are looking at is the *vendor's* judgment of an event's importance. It does not account for variables in your environment. Those variables can alter the weighting drastically. Here is where context is vital. What a vendor categorizes as a high-priority event may effectively be, in your organization's environment, only a mid-priority level 4 or 5 event. An event the vendor categorizes as low severity may be far more serious to you after you add context to it.

For example, a remote access trojan (RAT) is typically considered a level 5 or "major" event by many vendors, not a critical or high-priority event. It's considered of medium importance because the vendor has seen it before or considers it detectable. RATs typically provide administrative-level functionality to an external source (usually a threat actor) outside the organization, which makes a RAT extremely concerning to me as an analyst. Considering the scope of damage a threat actor could cause with administrative functionality over a device, I'd want that alert or event re-classified as critical, high-priority, or level 9 or 10.

Most vendors and products I've seen do not allow you to change the severity assigned to an events. If a product or platform has correlation capability, you may be able to control the level of severity assigned to a correlated alert or event for which you define the conditions. You still can't change the severity assigned by the vendor to a base alert/event or dependency alert/event.

With detection products that are based on signatures or rules, you can write, customize or add to vendor-provided content. In the signature or rule for the content, you can control the weighting or severity of the content. Here is an example of one way to write an open-source Snort IDS rule:

```
alert tcp $EXTERNAL_NET any -> 192.168.3.0/24 80
(msg:"testing alert used for security operations book";
pcre:"/GET.*\.htm/i"; classtype: web-http-activity;
reference:url, https://www.fireeye.com/blog/threat-research/2018/06/rig-
ek-delivering-monero-miner-via-propagate-injection-technique.html;
sid:9991001; rev:1;)
```

In the example, **classtype**, according to Snort documentation, "is used to categorize a rule as detecting an attack that is part of a more general type of attack class. Snort provides a default set of attack classes that are used by the default set of rules it provides. Defining classifications for rules provides a way to better organize the event data Snort produces". You can add, edit, or delete classtypes in the default set of attack classes. Figure 37 shows a partial list of attack classes, along with their description and assigned priority (http://manual-snort-org.s3-website-us-east-1.amazonaws.com/node31.html)

Table: Snort Default Classifications

Classtype	Description	Priority
attempted-admin	Attempted Administrator Privilege Gain	high
attempted-user	Attempted User Privilege Gain	high
inappropriate-content	Inappropriate Content was Detected	high
policy-violation	Potential Corporate Privacy Violation	high

Figure 37: Snort attack classes

To add a new custom attack class to Snort's classification.config file, defined according to Snort's documentation, the classtype needs to match the following format:

```
config classification:  <class name>,<class description>,<default
priority>
```

We could add something like this:

```
trojan-activity, Known Remote Access Trojan, High
```

The Snort signature or rule would look like this:

```
Alert tcp $HOME_NET any -> $EXTERNAL_NET $HTTP_PORTS (msg:"alert vbs rat";
```

```
flow:established,to_server; content:"some.website.net"; http_header;
fast_pattern:only; pcre:"/Host\x3A[^\r\n]*some\.website\.net/H";
classtype:trojan-activity; sid:9991002; rev:1;)
```

Context Across Multiple Products

Adding context from multiple products can enrich the alerts or events you're analyzing, as with correlation and SIEMs. (I write more about this in the next chapter.) Unfortunately, not enough organizations have skilled, experienced and knowledgeable correlation writers or content providers to write the logic or work out the scripts and integration successfully. Another challenge is that vendor A may not integrate well with vendor B without some type of security operations platform to bridge the gap. A third challenge is building on collection and correlation by taking actions and verifying or validating the results.

Every time you must pivot to another product or resource, your focus is distracted, time is wasted, and the chance of an error increases.

A common example is time format. One product may log or record/capture time as follows:

07JUL18 3:21pm

Contextual alerts may be in another product that uses a different time format:

07/07/2018 1521 hrs

Most security teams they do their best to align everything with UTC. Analysts in environments where time issues were severe have written their own Python scripts to ingest logs in JSON or CSV format and rewrite all dates and timestamps into a single format before they attempted to analyze anything.

Another scenario is shown in Figure 38:

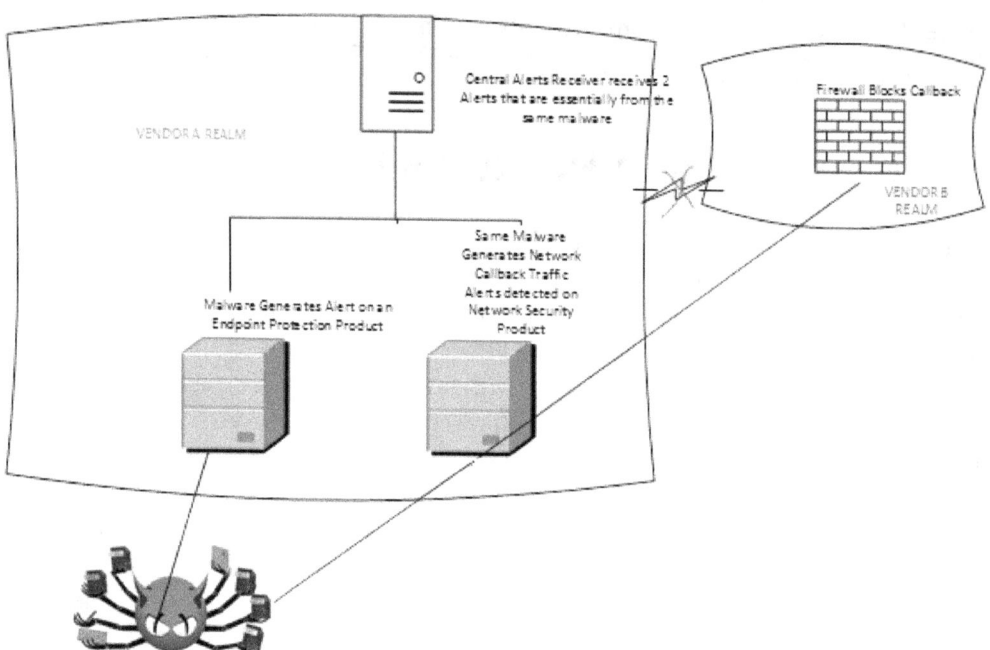

Figure 38: Lack of integration between products

A malware object is deployed from a malicious Visual Basic macro in a Word document. The object is detected and alerts are generated on an endpoint security device and on a separate network security device from vendor A. Both alerts are sent to a central alerts receiver, also from vendor A. The alert generated from the endpoint security device has no severity assigned. The alert from the network security device is assigned severity 7. Meanwhile, callbacks from the malware are blocked upstream at one of the organization's firewalls, which comes from vendor B.

The problem is that products from vendor A don't communicate with those from vendor B. This might seem OK, because the firewall is blocking callbacks. But when the malware object becomes polymorphic and changes certain characteristics, the firewall may no longer block it. Further, there is no common standard for weighting. What vendor A considers a severity 7 alert, vendor B might consider merely an observable event. The central alerts receiver from vendor A has no context outside its realm.

If there were communication between vendor A and vendor B and automation or scripted logic were deployed, the following might happen:

1. The firewall would notify the central alerts receiver of a blocking event.
2. The central alerts receiver would dynamically adjust the severity of the alert generated from the network security device to a severity 2. The blocking by the firewall reduced the threat to a level considered non-actionable.

Context in Restricted Environments

Problems with context can be amplified by regulatory requirements and in highly secure environments. For instance, in defense contracting, most governments and militaries deal with multiple networks, domains or enclaves based on security/secrecy classification. Incidents and details that occur at one level of classification must be moved to a higher classification, which is on a different network. Your security operations team cannot find, acquire, analyze and report or track an incident on a single network. Moving data is time consuming and liable to error. Policies based on regulations such as HIPAA, PCI, and GDPR affect workflow similarly.

Object Context—When Threat Actors Use Admin Resources Maliciously

This scenario has played out more and more over the past few years and will continue to be a challenge in the future. Threat actors want to blend in with normal behavior. One way of accomplishing this is to use administrative resources to facilitate their malicious goals. In a Microsoft environment, these resources include:

- PowerShell
- Windows Management Instrumentation
- Command-line utilities
- Scripts and macros such as Wscript.exe and Visual Basic scripts

Because the same resources are used with non-malicious intent by administrators, misuse isn't easy to detect. The technique of using built-in operating system resources for malicious purposes is known as "living off the land." FireEye has published blogs on threat actor groups – FIN7 being one of them—that employ exactly these tactics:

https://www.fireeye.com/blog/threat-research/2017/04/fin7-phishing-lnk.html

Some of this malware consists of several individual scripts that are each benign on their own. If you ran them individually into an object analyzer, from a single-scope functionality, they would be deemed benign or non-malicious. However, when they are strung together to run as a unit, they create memory resident objects of malicious functionality. After they run, they dissolve as memory-resident applications instantly or after a reboot or power cycle, until the next time the scripts are set to run. Unless you were scraping memory or doing constant detection in memory for malicious behavior of objects, you wouldn't detect this malware.

Examples of Incomplete Context

This section provides examples, using open-source products, of the challenges we have making informed and reasonable decisions with insufficient context. I don't want to criticize specific vendors or products; all have strengths and deficiencies. Many information/cyber security products rely on data from databases, logs, agents, connectors, collectors, packets, and so on. What one company focuses on, another company may not. Firewalls typically work on connection or session data available at various levels of the OSI stack. The same applies to IDS and IPS systems—they are driven by packets. In the following examples, some of the source data was never available in the packets to begin with.

As we explore where context could be added, ask your colleagues or your team to do a quick assessment of where they must jump around, dig for answers or lack context. Identifying those gaps is the first step to address the problems around context.

Firewalls

Figure 39 is a screenshot from a FreeBSD-based Open Source Firewall and Routing application called OPNSense. This application is covered by the Simplified BSD License, also known as the FreeBSD License:

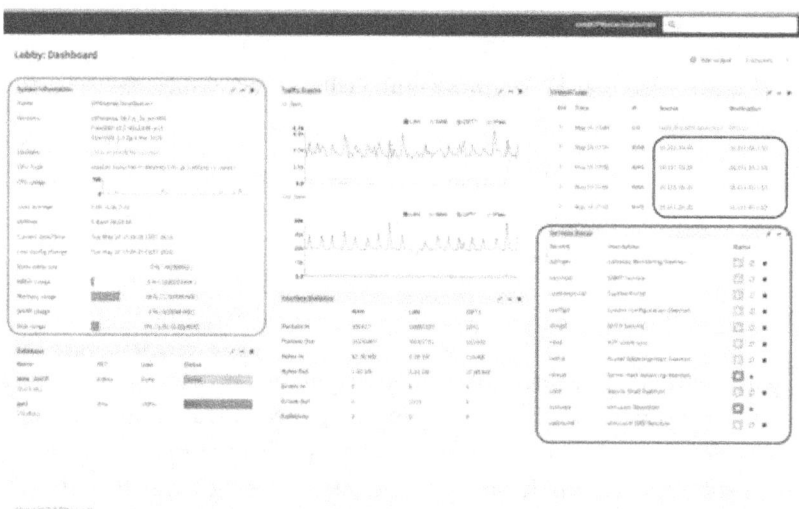

Figure 39: OPNSense

- The top-right oval shows source and destination addresses – but there is no context about what assets those addresses represent. Are they laptops? Desktops? Servers? There are no hostnames that would provide an idea of their location or role within an organization.

- The lower-right oval shows a list of services and whether they have been started– but there is no context as to what those services impact, or what network they provide services for. It looks like this is the scope of a single firewall. Do other firewalls provide backup or secondary services when these services are down? If so, shouldn't we be using something like a central firewall manager?
- The left oval shows system information. This is great for an administrator. However, a firewall admin or analyst doesn't need to know most of this information. I only need to know which users or groups are impacted by services being down, and what applications depend on those services.
- Regarding threat level intelligence or indicators of compromise, are the logs from this firewall being routed to a platform that can add context about actionable and relevant threats? Can the logs be evaluated against threat and intel or IOCs from threat actors or methods of attack? Can I compare the state of my threats to others in the same industry to provide feedback to my higher-ups?
- What protocols can this firewall handle? Are we evaluating HTTPS, SSL or TLS sessions? What are we missing by not having visibility into other protocols?
- There is an option for adding widgets. Are there widgets that provide the context that I need? If not, how do I get data and telemetry out of this product and into a platform where I can shape the content, add the context I need, and have the flexibility required to do analysis?
- There appear to be no reporting capabilities here. What are our options for reporting? We need to get telemetry or data, alerts, events, alarms out of this and into a reporting system where we can create trends and various levels of reports for groups such as IT operations, security operations, executive groups, and risk managers.
- As new threat indicators or known artifacts become available, how do we evaluate those indicators or artifacts against prior data (retroactive alerting)? What is the retention time for logs and alerts generated from this product?
    - Do the retention times match regulations we are bound by or the requirements from our analytic and security operations team?
    - If (or when) we are audited, how likely are we will pass the audit?
- Regarding policy granularity on the firewall's access control lists, how dynamic are the ACLs? Are they binary in nature, either on or off, enabled or disabled? Is manual configuration required? Or can lists, rules, and policies be dynamically enabled or disabled for varying time ranges according to risk state? For example, if a popular website has malvertisement objects that we need to block, can we block just the stream of those malvertisements or do we need to block the entire site? Once the threat is resolved, do we have to manually disable control lists, rules or policies or can they be dynamically altered by automation or one of our security operations resources?

Intrusion Detection Event Manager

Figure 40 is a screenshot from Snorby, an open source application covered by the FSF/Free Software Foundation GNU license. This is an application and networking monitoring framework that can be integrated with open source Snort IDS:

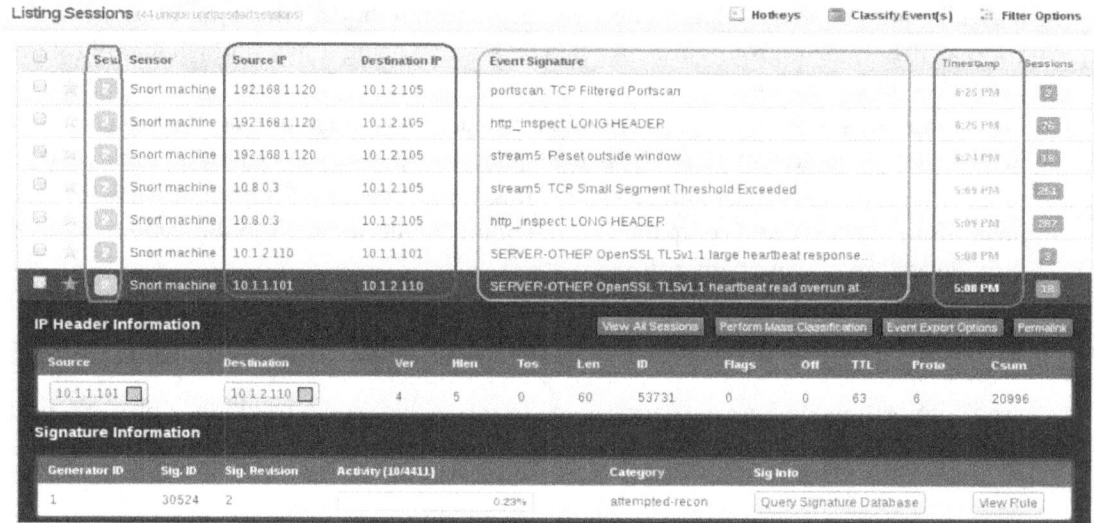

Figure 40: Snorby

- In the first oval, what does "severity 2" mean? This might be explained in the Snort or Snorby documentation, but without context, we don't know the effective/actual severity of an event the vendor labels "severity 2". (If it is the severity originating from the attack-class defined in the Snort signature, it will depend on who wrote the Snort signature)
- In the second oval, many of the same contextual issues identified with firewalls apply. There is no context about what asset belongs to those addresses, their host names, usernames, or the organization/department they belong to.
- In the third oval, these event descriptions were most likely sourced from the msg/message field included in the Snort signature or rule that matched packet traffic. Some might be descriptive enough (a port scan originating from IP 192.168.1.120), but others do not mean much without the context of what transpired before and after the packet that generated the alert. Without full packet capture context to include in analysis, which might need to be 15 minutes before or after (or more), there is insufficient context to understand events such as **stream5: reset outside window** or **http_inspect: Long Header.**
- In the fourth oval, the timestamp is somewhat vague. Was it the time the alert was received by Snorby? Was it the time the alert was generated on the sensor? Is there a difference between the time when the packet was evaluated the time when the sensor

alerted? Those two may not be the same due to many reasons, such as objects queued for submission to busy detection engines.

Packet Analysis

Figure 41 is a screenshot we previously used from WireShark. This application is covered under the GNU General Public License version 2:

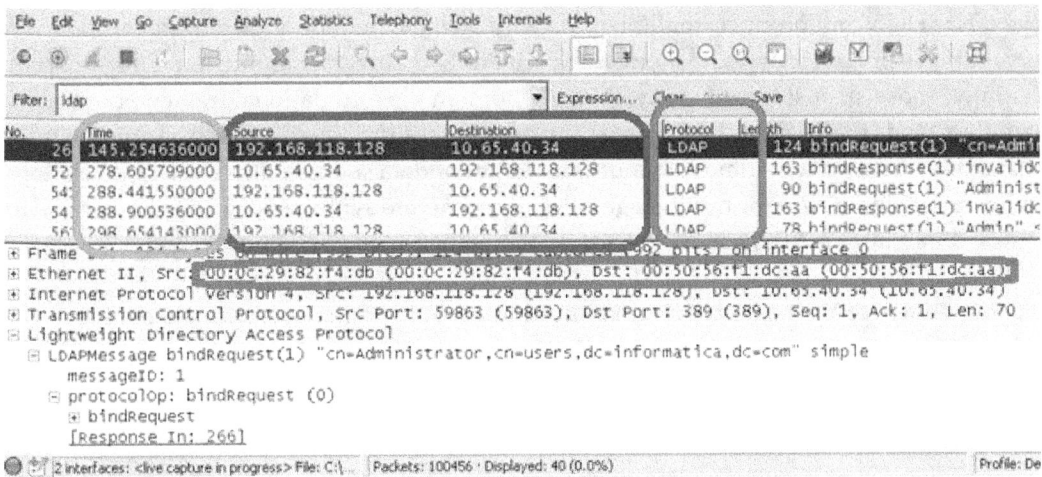

Figure 41: WireShark

- In the middle oval, many of the same contextual issues identified before apply. There is no context about what asset belongs to those addresses, their host names, usernames, or the organization/department they belong to.
- In the right oval, are these considered excessive numbers of LDAP BIND requests? If so, why? If not, are they normal for the version of LDAP that is deployed on the network?
- In the left oval, although the field is titled "Time", these don't look like any normal timestamps. In Wireshark, this number shows how many seconds passed from the time the packet capture was submitted to WireShark. The first event we see is frame 26, 145.254 seconds from when the packet capture was started. When was the packet capture recorded (based on the file system date/timestamp on the .PCAP file) and in what context was the PCAP taken?
- In the bottom oval, what network interface card (NIC) are those MAC addresses assigned to? The first 3 octets are an organization identifier (OID) identifying the manufacturer. The last 3 octets are a unique identifier assigned to that NIC. As an analyst, you may need to know who manufactured a NIC, whether it is virtual, whether it is on the main board (typical of a laptop) or an external NIC that might be on a desktop or a server.

Contextually Aware Security Operations Platforms

There is no single answer to the problem. However, platforms are available that were designed from the ground up to help reduce the gaps or dissolve the deficiencies relating to lack of context. If you engage with a one-platform, single-scope or narrowly focused multiple-scope vendor, they may introduce more context deficiencies than they can resolve. Your future options will be limited, and you'll run out of runway with them sooner than you think.

FireEye offers Helix and products that integrate with Helix to help provide additional context to your event types or data sources. Among them are FireEye Threat Analytics and FireEye Security Orchestrator, those are just two of many. Helix is built on the foundational framework required to adapt to thousands of different data sources and event types ("classes" in Helix terminology), tens of thousands of fields to accommodate multiple classes of data sources, and a rules/correlation system to create single-stage or multi-stage rules that generate synthetic/correlated events. Along with those capabilities is a built-in incident management and case handling system.

A major advantage of Helix is that you don't need to rip out and replace your current security operations resources. Figure 42 shows that Helix can integrate with various FireEye platforms and products as well as enterprise products and systems (EPS) resources:

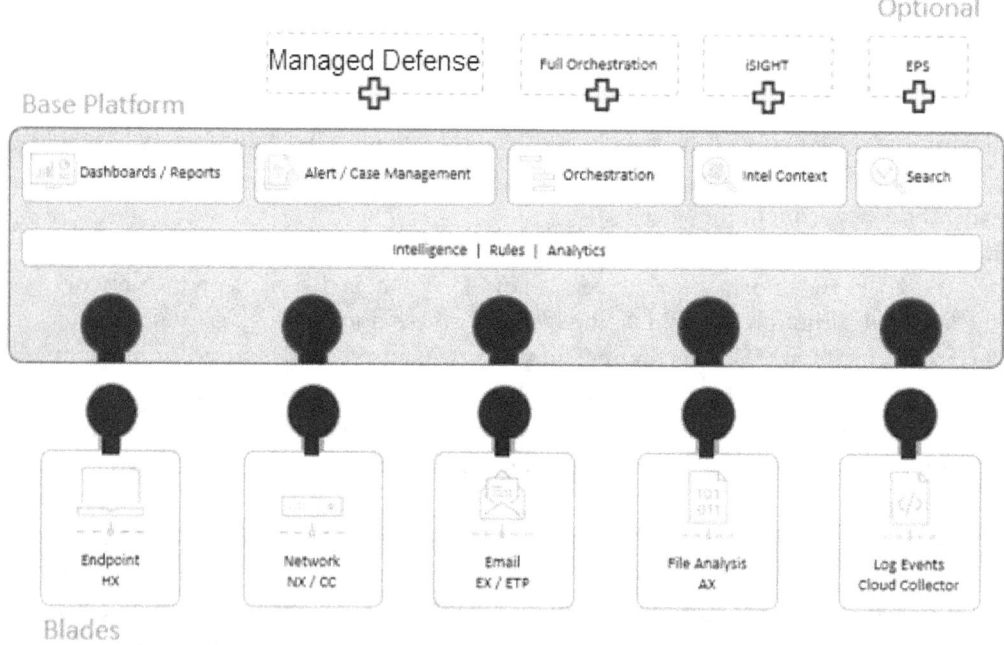

Figure 42: Helix integration

Plenty of resources describe Helix better than I can here. Go to FireEye's main web page and navigate to Solutions, Enterprise Security and Helix: https://www.fireeye.com/solutions/helix.html

Other companies may offer data analytics, big data products or various resources by different names and terms.

Chapter 8: Security Orchestration, Automation, and Response—SOAR

Over a professional career in information/cyber security, I remember what geologists call "tectonic shifts" within the industry. In the mid-2000s, new compliance regulations in the US and overseas drove many organizations into the arms of Enterprise Security Management (ESM—also called SEM: Security Event Management, SIM: Security Information Management or Security Incident Management, and SIEM: Security Information and Event Management). Although ESM existed before, this was a major shift.

Another tectonic shift was dynamic analysis and sandboxing. Before sandboxing, dynamic analysis was a very labor- and time-intensive task that was highly susceptible to errors. I had been using open-source sandboxing resources like Cuckoo and Anubis with limited success. Mainstream dynamic analysis companies started forming in 2002-2004 time and really caught on in 2006–2007.

I think that the next information/cyber security tectonic movement will be with Security Orchestration, Automation and Response (SOAR). While not an easy or light set of functions and capabilities, the long-term advantages and scalability that organizations can achieve with SOAR easily outweigh the challenges during the first months of planning, deployment and implementation.

This chapter discusses what SOAR can do, some use cases, and topics to consider when you bring in a SOAR platform. We'll also tie in FireEye's platform for SOAR , Security Orchestrator (SO).

What SOAR Is

SOAR at its heart is orchestration that enables smart response. There is no doubt that your organization is doing automation using scripting to interact with application programming interfaces. In the information technology or security business, this is often referred to as "wiring together" apps. SOAR *integrates* orchestration with automation. A SOAR product or platform enables your security operations team by automating many mundane, routine, frequently required manual processes that support broader incident response and analysis. It allows you to insert a decision point or junction that requires human interaction at any point. This orchestration and automation takes some of the load off analysts, allowing them to devote more time to critical thinking.

SOAR can do things like take indicators of compromise from your FireEye Network Security platform, run them directly through VirusTotal, and display results in reports and dashboards.

For example, the following tasks, which I do on 80% of the alerts that I see, could be easily automated:

- Check an IP address with IPVoid (http://www.ipvoid.com/)
- Check a URL address with URLVoid (http://www.urlvoid.com/)
- Send an MD5 hash to VirusTotal (https://www.virustotal.com/)
- Send a malicious object from an endpoint agent-based product to the FireEye AX Malware Analysis System
- Submit an ASCII string to multiple decoders and return results (something like http://www.asciitohex.com)

More complex tasks can include the following:

- Assign incidents to a particular analyst based on certain criteria
- Live Response actions such as collecting all processes or all network connections from a target machine
- Collect target objects (such as processes, files, or folders) and run appropriate analysis tools automatically (for example, hashing all processes)

Caveats of SOAR

SOAR should not be considered just another security operations resource on the same level as your IDS, IPS, firewalls, and so on. If your SOAR becomes another alert and event generator creating audible alarms and email notifications, it will simply add to the avalanche of alerts and events.

SOAR is not a replacement for human analysts. A SOAR product or platform is not a head count reducer. Your security operations team needs enablement—the right tools for the right job. SOAR allows you to use your limited human resources more effectively. A truly functional, deeply integrated and fully operational SOAR does not replace a SOC—it increases capacity and becomes a trusted resource that elevates the analytic workflow of professionals on the security team.

Test a SOAR product thoroughly before you buy it. First-generation and second-generation SOAR products had significant usability issues. Rule-based access control (RBAC) and authentication were flaky, requiring admins to reset connections or restart services and daemons multiple times per day. Regex statements in Python scripts were faulty. XML parsers worked great during evaluations but flopped due to incompatibilities in a production environment. Stability was also an issue with some early SOAR products. Kernel panics could happen as often as every 5-10 minutes due to heavy latency on back-end systems. Unstable logic engines that worked great with light automation fell apart under heavy orchestration loads. Most products and platforms run differently under light conditions during evaluations or in training environments than in production, heavy use conditions.

If you are considering SOAR or thinking about the parameters to conduct a proof of concept/proof of value, be prepared to put the product or platform you are considering through its paces. That may not be the easiest thing to do in a pre-sales environment. Some organizations engage with third-party, vendor-agnostic advisors and consultants that have experience asking the tough questions that require product and platform analysis under load, various use case build-outs, and so on. Sometimes the use of traffic or log generators rolling at various speeds to test scoping is required. Ask critical questions and validate the answers under various loads and conditions before you sign on the dotted line.

Orchestration and Automation Use Cases

Here are a few use cases or scenarios that a SOAR platform, such as FireEye Security Orchestrator, can handle:

Light Orchestration

1. Ingest an alert generated by a SIEM or Threat Analytics Platform.
2. Cross-reference indicators from the alert (IP address and hostname) against the Windows Event Manager from the system or systems generating the alert. This step validates that the event was logged at the endpoint to ensure that the alert is not a false positive.
3. Run an automated data acquisition from HX or a Live Response Script from another vendor's endpoint detection product to gather data for deeper analysis.
4. Extract the results of the data acquisition or live response script from a compressed format to text, JSON or XML format and present them to an analyst for further action.

Heavier Orchestration

1. An endpoint agent detects a suspicious behavior in a virtual host running as an Amazon machine instance (AMI) under AWS.
2. An automated response workflow connects to a logging service in AWS via API and launches a playbook that is integrated with your production routing infrastructure.

3. The first course of action in the playbook changes the instance of the deployed AMI system to a contained or quarantined subnet, VLAN or " dirty net".

4. With integration back to your endpoint platform, an automated process begins a disk or memory acquisition, or both, on the suspect AMI.

5. Evidence is copied from the suspect system to a forensics storage node in the cloud that is only accessible by the security team and protected with encryption.

6. The machine instance or deployed image is rolled back and validated to a known, clean state. (Alternatively, the results are presented to an analyst for manual intervention.)

SOAR Planning and Challenges

Security Orchestration typically starts with the definition of specifications or tasks that you want to orchestrate and automate. Those could be simply a few pages of process flow or detailed flowcharts. Tasks can also be defined from other resources such as video recordings, audio recordings of conference calls, or collaboration sessions between your security operations team and an SO engineer/content creator.

A challenge of planning security orchestration is that our platform is like a Swiss army knife; it can do many things. You can orchestrate processes that facilitate better integration between resources, but you can orchestrate bad or faulty processes just as easily. Some organizations aren't prepared for the challenges of implementing SOAR because they are more familiar with inline products that work with minimal setup and are faster to deploy in production.

SIEMs have often been characterized by "puppy syndrome". Puppies are cute, furry, cuddly and are easy to fall in love with. Puppies also require training and a long-term commitment to nurturing and growth if they are to become well-trained adult dogs. Likewise, SOAR has powerful capabilities but requires planning and testing that can be very labor-intensive. You can't ignore your SOAR product or platform or let it coast long term. It requires a commitment of resources, time, dedication and use to be practical and useful for your team.

Getting from the needs and requirements phase to building logic trees, decision points, courses of action and playbooks isn't a short process, either. Orchestration and automation requires understanding what your organization needs, lining up the resources to facilitate access to systems that you need, and having developers available to provide specifications for APIs. Those APIs need to support queries and actions relating to products and platforms that are already in house. Sometimes that is easier said than done.

Sensible Points for Human Interaction

A SOAR can automate various actions and responses, but you don't have to create your playbooks or courses of action that way. You can build in stop or junction points that require human interaction. You choose the points for human interaction that are sensible for your organization. I tend to be cautious with anything that could stop communications, inhibit business productivity or generally cause pain to reflect in my direction.

Digitizing the flow

You need to transform the process flow that your security operations team follows into a digital representation of tasks, actions, decision points, and so on. For example, you may have the following tasks, flow and decisions:

1. Analyst A triages an alert and escalates to Analyst B.
2. Analyst B adds context to the alert from 5- 7 different resources and escalates to Analyst C.
3. Analyst C validates the work of Analyst B and decides that memory should be captured from the endpoint that created the original alert.
4. Analyst C performs memory analysis and hands over all the information to Analyst D.
5. Analyst D creates a report and documents the incident in a ticketing or case management/workflow system.

We'll work that into a course of action for Security Orchestrator in the next few pages.

Planning For Errors, Stop Points, Loopbacks and Multiple Runs/Returns

With orchestration, there are more tasks and events to plan for than you probably handle today via scripting or single-threaded automation. While most scripts accommodate simple levels of errors or incorrect data handling conditions, orchestration tasks need to be able to accommodate more:

- Errors
- Data drops
- Stoppage points in task flows
- Loopback operations
- Extensive logic trees
- Multiple run/return operations where tasks are re-run two or three times. (Recall the dynamic malware in Chapter 4 that changes as it deploys from endpoint to endpoint. The only way to determine whether malware is static or dynamic is to run it multiple times and analyze the changes or deltas).

With a mature SOAR (at least the 3rd or 4th generation) that has a well-developed process for adding in tasks and logic operations, it is easy to set up automation tasks and simple, single-line courses of action or playbooks. It's harder to accommodate the wide range of "what if" scenarios that could break that simple course of action at any point.

FireEye Security Orchestrator

FireEye Security Orchestrator (SO) is an open workflow automation and orchestration platform that helps you improve response times, reduce risk exposure, and maintain process consistency across your security program. It unifies disparate technologies and incident handling processes into a single console that codifies experiences from the frontlines to deliver real-time guided responses. With over 140 plug-ins, definitions for devices and adapters, and a highly scalable and extensible ability to write courses of actions (referred to as playbooks), SO can save time, money, and resources. SO produces consistent and multilevel orchestrated tasks and actions running simultaneously throughout your security operations team.

SO integrates with both FireEye and third-party products and services to provide effective threat detection and incident responses tasks, actions and responses. The SO workflow builder allows you to model your security tactics, processes and procedures and provides an extensive plug-in API architecture for integrating external systems.

The next few sections show some parts of SO in action.

Plug-Ins

SO defines plug-ins as resources that we can either work with or send tasks to. Plug-ins, devices and adapters are the building blocks you use to automate courses of action in Security Orchestrator. They integrate SO with upstream and downstream systems by running commands to send and receive data. Figure 43 shows a partial list of the default plug-ins in a recent version of SO. The content can be customized, and custom plug-ins can also be written.

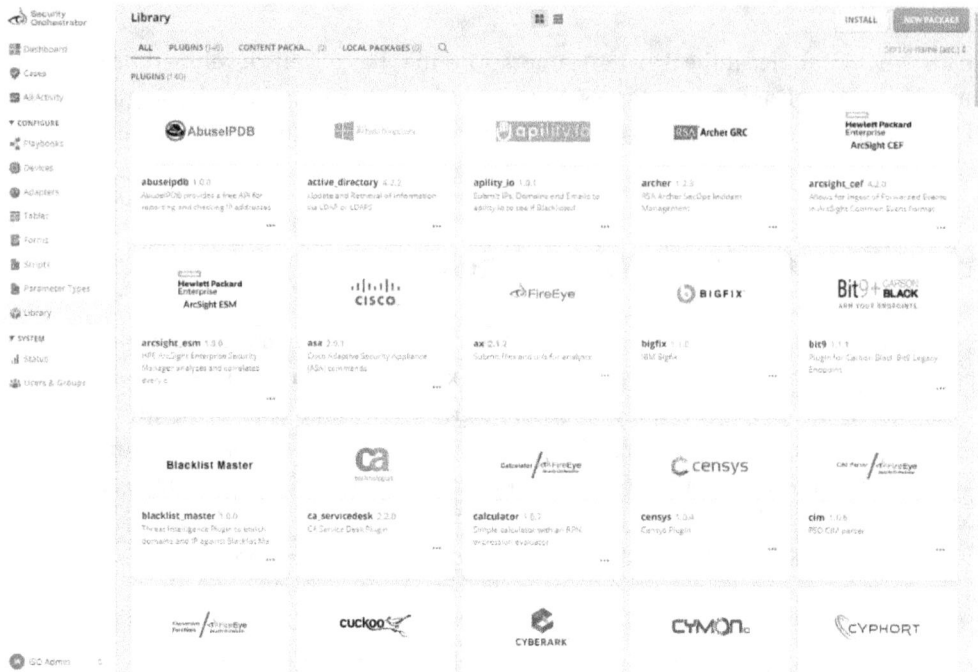

Figure 43: Plug-ins in SO

Figure 44 is a closer look at a plug-in for the AbuseIPDB database:

Figure 44: AbuseIP plug-in

A few of the functions that the 1.0.0 version of the AbuseIPDB Plug-in supports are shown in Figure 45:

Figure 45: AbuseIPDB plug-in functions

The set of functionalities that a single plug-in supports is called the package content.

Devices and Adapters

Devices represent the physical devices. Adapters define connections that can be made to individual devices. For instance, a device can be created to represent an NX Network Security platform or a group of firewalls. An adapter allows us to select a specific Network Security appliance, VX node or firewall. For instance, an adapter can be set up to address firewall 5 in a group of 10 firewalls. Once we know what is configurable through our plug-ins, we then create a device and configure it through device parameters. After we create devices, we create and configure adapters.

Courses of Action / Playbooks

A course of action (or playbook) is the task or set of tasks and orchestration that you want SO to engage in. A fully functional course of action based on tasks and actions defined in writing and developed into SO content looks something like Figure 46:

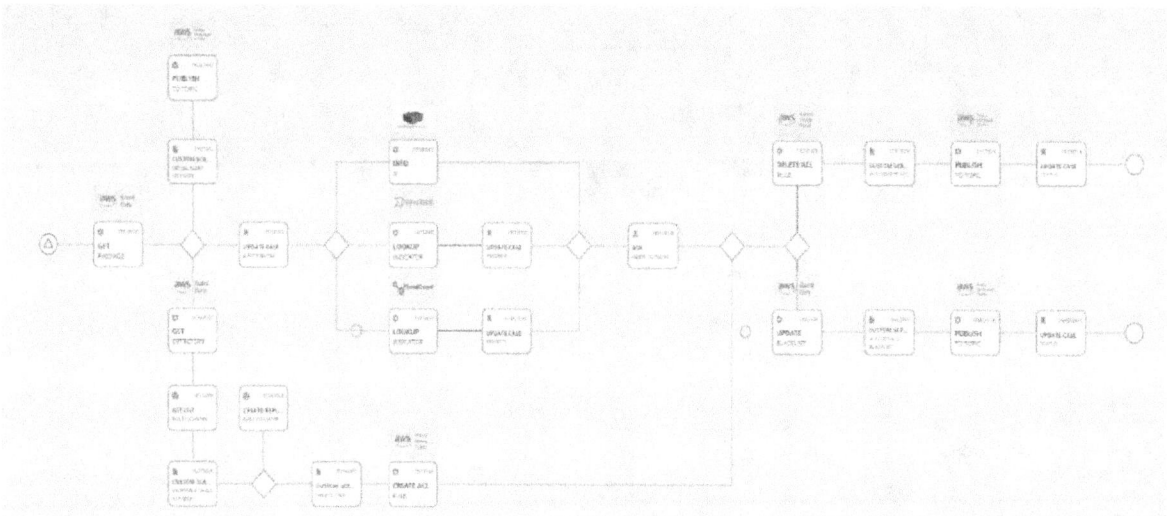

Figure 46: Course of Action

That might look like a bit of an eye chart, but the user interface to Security Orchestrator lets you zoom in and out. Everything typically starts with an adapter for a specific data source, represented by the following icon (Figure 47):

Figure 47: Adapter icon

From there, we define the tasks to engage in based on the capabilities of the adapter.

The orchestration case shown here is a course of action from a log ingestion sourced from AWS Guard Duty. At the beginning, an adapter receives log events from Guard Duty, which essentially are event identifiers. One task for automation is to match the event IDs with findings that we can feed into other tasks. That is represented by Figure 48:

Figure 48: Task in a course of action

As we work through the courses of action near the bottom, we get lists of IP addresses and create rules; run a script that increments the rule numbers; and implement those rules into a blocking action on an AWS firewall (Figure 49).

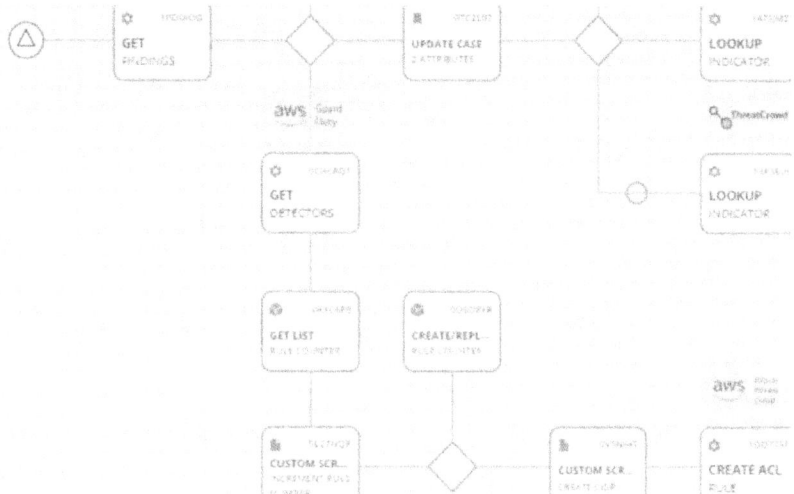

Figure 49: Course of action detail

At certain points in the course of action, this icon represents where we have inserted a manual check (Figure 50):

Figure 50: Manual check in a course of action

While we are working on some tasks, other tasks are running in parallel. We also have courses of action that check IP addresses as well as indicators from the AWS Guard Logs against VirusTotal and ThreatCrowd. The results of these checks are added to incident/case details and presented to an analyst for manual analysis before action is taken (Figure 51).

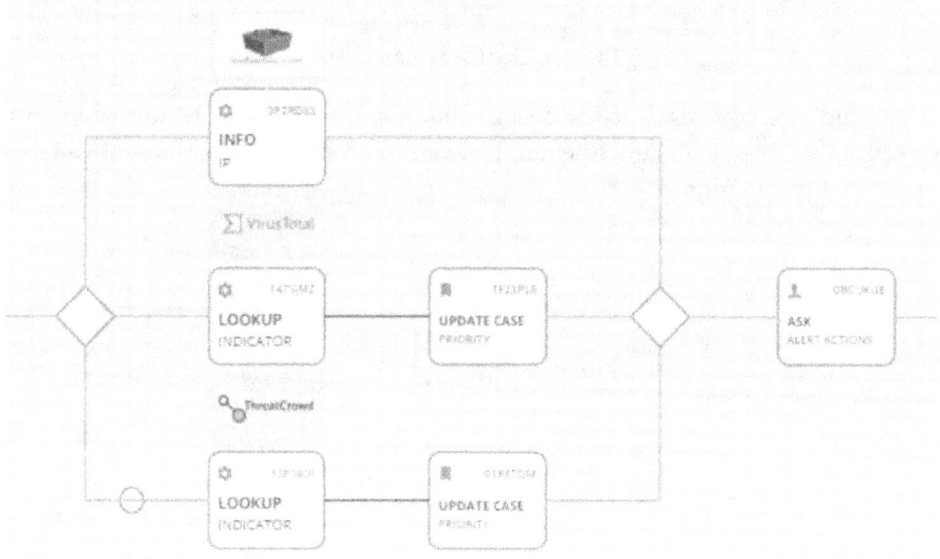

Figure 51: Presenting results to analyst

In the above course of action, you can see several tasks, actions and playbook operations. Orchestration encompasses the scope of several activities. For your seasoned analysts, the time saving and reduction in manual and laborious tasks are evident. Now all they need to do is act on the decision point that is the result of orchestration. For analysts who are less experienced or new to the team, this allows them to technically analyze beyond their knowledge/skill level, or, to use a boxing analogy, to "fight above their weight class".

Phases of SOAR Deployment and Integration

Here are the four phases of SOAR deployment:

1. Planning
    - Task definitions, documentation, automation tasks detailed in local or programmatic steps.

- With Security Orchestrator, this includes researching available plug-ins, matching them to the version of the resource you want to integrate, and preparing for creation and configuration of devices and adapters.

2. Content creation, testing, tweaking
   - Set up tasks, automations, courses of actions, and playbooks.
   - Run them repeatedly until you validate that your course of action does what you expect.

3. Security team left seat / right seat
   - While your security team continues to work normally, you run the course of action and orchestration and then compare results. Your analyst team compares their work to what orchestration did.
   - Next, the orchestration runs completely on its own and then your team validates that the work orchestration accomplished was correct and appropriate.

4. Acceptance and Maintenance
   - You have a level of confidence in your SO platform. You have a moderate to extensive library of content and courses of actions running simultaneously with little to no effort and producing valuable tasks, actions, orchestration and response. Now you grow from here.
   - SO needs maintenance, updating, content creation and revision; hence the need for an administrator or SOAR engineer.

Your Security Orchestration Engineer

Your deployment of Security Orchestration will require a senior admin or, in some cases, a dedicated engineer. If you don't have the in-house resources for an SO engineer, there are multiple alternatives. One alternative is that FireEye can run your deployment of Security Orchestrator through our Managed Defense organization, long term, short term or through "surge support" as your business requires. Another alternative is that FireEye can assign a Designated Support Engineer (DSE) specifically to the support, administration and maintenance of your SO deployment. FireEye also offers training.

Some of the tasks of a senior administrator or SO engineer are:

- Maintaining, updating and revising plug-ins
- Creating, maintaining and updating tasks and orchestrations/playbooks
- Backing up and testing restoration operations of your SO deployment
- Documenting, testing and providing reports on performance and telemetry from SO
- Creating, maintaining and updating content within SO
- Creating, maintaining and updating devices and adapters within SO

- Over-the-shoulder or informal knowledge transfer to your admins, engineers, support staff, analysts, incident responders/handlers and security operations team
- Working with external vendors regarding their APIs and plug-ins to ensure that credentials are maintained, connections are active and available, and so on when versions change.

More Benefits of SOAR

Metrics

Your higher-ups will not only expect results from your SOAR platform—they will want tangible metrics that they can use to justify the organization's growth and demonstrate a return on investment. The metrics displayed on the dashboard include "time saved by plugin" as well as "time saved by command". You can define metrics while you are creating content in SO, and SO will dynamically track them and display them on the main dashboard. There are other points within the platform for extraction of telemetry and statistics that can be used in reports and trends, or routed outside to a reporting package.

Higher Levels of Confidence

When your platform is mature, has been put through its paces, and has an extensive library of courses of actions and orchestrations that have run successfully, you can increase the level of confidence in your security operations execution as well as in your analytic workflow. Most organizations outside government and the military don't have the resources to have incidents or intrusions analyzed two or three times by multiple analysts to increase confidence in the final reports. In fact, it's typically just the opposite. Most security operations teams are so inundated with alerts, events, alarms, and floods of information from various threat intelligence products (some of which may contradict each other), they barely have enough time for even one analyst to work an incident. SOAR can give you higher levels of confidence in the work that you do.

Leveraging SOAR to Fill a Critical Live Response Gap

One methodology for incident response/handling and analysis that we often recommend and have built entire products and platforms around is what we call Live Response. On the FireEye Endpoint Security Platform (HX), this commonly referred to as data acquisition or script acquisition. Live Response is modular, is often quick depending on how scripts are optimized and configured, and can be run against multiple endpoints at one time.

When the data or script acquisition runs, it returns results for a moment in time. As we saw in Chapter 2, you need to know normal and abnormal by comparing a control to a variable, which means collecting data sets to compare deltas. For instance, a collection script may include system information, a file and folder list running eight levels deep, and the same network details you would get by running netstat -anob. You can collect the three data components four times per day. However, comparing the four data sets for changes is time consuming and liable to error prone. This is where SOAR shines. Let the automation and orchestration do what computers do best— freeing your analysts and human capital to do their brain work.

Chapter 9: Incident Response in the Cloud

As many of us in information/cyber security have observed over the years, the priority for resources and innovative development is always IT, with security a distant second. With the rising rate of change and level of scalability that virtualization and cloud platforms provide, the ratio between those platforms and IS architecture or infrastructure is staggering. Most security operations organizations simply cannot keep pace. The only hope we have of catching up is to dynamically integrate virtualization and cloud platform providers with security operations resources at all levels. If your security operations team attempts to copy and paste your current IR/IH processes from an on-premise, physical presence under your control to a set of cloud platform providers and expects them to work the same way, you are in for some long days. I've never heard of a seamless transition.

The advantages of cloud and virtual deployments are well known, including:

- Automated provisioning of endpoints, networks and resources
- No-downtime deployments
- Ease of monitoring multiple deployments within a virtual cluster or specific cloud provider
- Agile environment to fail fast, break often and fail at will
- Automated build and testing and faster speed allow you to run multiple scenarios for configurations, quality assurance, and stability factoring

Less well known is that many of the traditional information security requirements still apply to virtual and cloud environments, and they are amplified dramatically. The scale and speed with which virtual networks and endpoints can be created and dismantled means that changes can happen in minutes to hours, not weeks to months. With every change, we need to consider how to integrate firewalls, anti-virus/malware products, static and dynamic detection platforms, IDS/IPS, and all our other security resources.

These are just a few of the "traditional" information security requirements that apply to virtual and cloud environments:

- Logging and event monitoring
- Anomaly detection
- Access control and integration with monitoring, detection and security resources
- Ingress/egress controls, such as virtual firewalls or proxies, and integration with security resources

- Configuration and patch management
- User and privilege management
- Vulnerability assessment and management
- Endpoint/agent rapid deployment, provisioning and decommissioning
- Ability to dynamically query and retrieve host details at all levels (hardware, operating system, applications)
- Ability to audit a cloud provider's essential security measures just as you would with a physical asset

Virtual environments bring additional new requirements as well.

This chapter highlights the common challenges, use cases and best business practices to consider around incident response and handling in the age of virtualization and cloud providers. It also provides recommendations for revising your security operations incident response and handling processes to accommodate virtual environments in general and issues common to most cloud providers.

This chapter does not take a deep dive into virtualization environments such as VMWare, Oracle Virtual Box, Microsoft Hypervisor, and so on, or the cloud platforms of Amazon Web Services, Microsoft Azure, or Oracle Cloud Infrastructure. You'll need to investigate individual virtualization vendors and cloud providers on your own. One chapter on this topic can't be enough because there is always something new to learn.

Security Concerns with Cloud Providers

Many old-timers in IT raise an eyebrow and smile at the term "cloud computing" because they recall the decades of mainframes and time-sharing systems, and the pain of figuring out where data center applications, resources, storage arrays and so on were located, let alone managing them. I taught at Hewlett-Packard facilities in California in the late 1990s that had little signs posted by the telephones that read: "Do not disconnect this telephone from the wall. Connections will be disabled, and the phones are controlled & reset from a telecommunications center in Atlanta, Georgia". If someone disconnected the phone from the wall socket and disrupted connections, the IT department in that location was neither responsible for the problem nor authorized to fix it. With cloud providers, your IT infrastructure is not within the same company and the physical location of an endpoint might not even be in your own country. This section addresses some security concerns that are particularly important with cloud providers.

Memory Capture and Disk Imaging on Cloud Assets

The task of capturing objects, challenging enough in your own network, is compounded in the cloud. Unfortunately, not many organizations realize this until the fire is upon them. The mechanics of taking a memory image or getting a hard disk image from a cloud virtual system or machine instance may be very different. You may not even have the administrative capability to do so. Issues with latency, inconsistent connectivity, and insufficient bandwidth to grab large objects are more severe in cloud environments. Always run a table-top exercise and assess each task thoroughly before a live, production-level incident occurs.

Different Structures and Terminology

It's the same problem we see among vendors, certification groups and industry groups. Every virtualization environment vendor and cloud provider has its own structure and its own terminology, acronyms, standards, and so on. What one vendor calls a firewall another might call a "container control". What one provider calls a "machine instance" another calls a "Virtual PC". The dizzying array of terms only complicates the journey.

Attackers Use Your Own Cloud Platforms Against You

It could be as simple as some credentials inadvertently included in a script posted publicly on GitHub. Or perhaps a store of admin/root credentials embedded in a payload file that was uploaded to an online resource. Threat actors can find these credentials and use them to gain administrative or root-level privileges in your cloud or virtual environment. From there, they can spin up a virtual PC or machine instance, do some bad things, then tear it down undetected. This is especially hard to detect with VMs or cloud machines spinning up and down so rapidly. A virtual administrator or cloud support team may be tracking VM or machine instance statistics, but that data may not make it to your security team.

One hunting technique is to look for the instances when one endpoint is maintaining communications to several outbound IPs at the same time, and vice versa. If those connections seem to persist over hours or days, they may indicate malware engaged in connectivity to multiple C2 servers. (However, multi-session streaming is very popular with media and content platforms such as NetFlix and YouTube, as well as adware servers.)

Unclear Division of Responsibilities

Although most cloud providers provide tools to help enable security monitoring within their own environment, analysis and incident response are still your organization's responsibility. The provider's primary responsibility typically extends to detection and protection of their cloud across multiple deployments with multiple customers. Primary responsibility for your organization lies with you. Most cloud providers have three categories of tasks and responsibilities for information security:

- Tasks for which the cloud provider is responsible
- Tasks for which the customer or subscriber is responsible
- Tasks and responsibilities shared between the provider and the customer or subscriber

Among all the contracts, statements of work, and service-level agreements should be explicit documentation of all tasks and responsibilities. That documentation should be signed by a director or high-level executive in your company and in the provider's organization. There *cannot* be any ambiguity. If a task or responsibility is not explicitly assigned, when push comes to shove, the task will not get done.

Division of responsibility extends to ownership and access. It's a common misconception that the customer owns virtual machines and their contents. In fact, cloud providers *are not* required to provide you access to virtual machines, unless it is specifically included in an agreement. Unfortunately, agreements between your company and the cloud provider typically aren't signed at the security operations level. Don't assume that the VMs are your property or that you have full access.

Recent Cloud-Related Incidents

The examples in this section all come from open source reporting and I'll make sure to provide the links to where you can read more about their details. Although some did not originate in the cloud, they all involved cloud platforms, sites or resources at one point or another. Credentials have been discovered in open drop box accounts, open shares that were accessible from the internet were hosted on endpoints deployed through various cloud providers, and so on. Company intellectual property, passkeys, schematics and architecture documents, code repositories and generally sensitive data has been inadvertently documented in presentations or documents hosted on websites deployed by a cloud provider. Once threat actors have discovered those resources, it's relatively easy for them to access those resources from cloud-based platforms that have not been secured or defended properly. I've even seen cloud-hosted media files such as conference call recordings and internal company webcasts, objects like video drivers or python scripts that contained clear text credentials to VPNs, FTP sites or open shares that should not be externally accessible (but were).

Here are a few notable cloud related incidents from the past few years:

- OneLogin https://www.onelogin.com/blog/may-31-2017-security-incident
  - Cloud provider involved: Amazon Web Services
- Uber https://www.theguardian.com/technology/2017/nov/21/uber-data-hack-cyber-attack
  - Cloud provider involved: Amazon Web Services
- US Central Command (CENTCOM) & US Pacific Command (PACOM)
  https://www.upguard.com/breaches/cloud-leak-centcom
  - Cloud provider involved: Amazon Web Services
- US Intelligence Command (INSCOM) https://www.upguard.com/breaches/cloud-leak-inscom
  - Cloud provider involved: Amazon Web Services
- Accenture https://www.zdnet.com/article/accenture-left-a-huge-trove-of-client-passwords-on-exposed-servers/
  - Cloud provider involved: Amazon Web Services
- Tesla http://www.eweek.com/cloud/tesla-cloud-account-data-breach-revealed-in-redlock-security-report
  - Cloud provider involved: Amazon Web Services
- Deloitte https://www.wired.com/story/security-news-of-the-week-deloitte-sonic-whole-foods-breach/
  - Cloud provider involved: Microsoft Azure
- John's Hopkins University Applied Physics Laboratory
  https://aws.amazon.com/blogs/publicsector/building-a-cloud-specific-incident-response-plan/
  - Cloud provider involved: Amazon Web Services

The root causes of these breaches, compromises and incidents range from poor operational security to "loose fingers" to straight-up malicious intent.

We've highlighted pain points like having too much to do, too little resources, being pressed for results or in a rush to analyze and work through incidents. It is not uncommon for objects to be submitted to various online resources that might have provided a quick "free" (it's never free) answer but resulted in the submitter losing control over the object. In these cases, mistakes happen, and inadvertent disclosures or loss of data would be considered unintentional. The problem is, whether intentional or not, the result is the same.

I've seen organizations attempt to rationalize between the intentional and unintentional. One such organization considered compromised data that was released on a network of lower classification as a "data spill". As soon as you even whispered the words "data spill", you might as well clear your morning or afternoon for the onslaught of regulatory paperwork, forms, approvals, collection of spilled data or assessment of scoping, notification of owners and recipients, and so on. This became such an elevated level of effort that the term "data splash" started gaining popularity to mean the "unintentional/accidental disclosure or release of data in small quantities". The perception was that a splash wasn't as bad as a formal spill. I still shake my head thinking about that. To a professional in the information/cyber security business, you don't get "a little" in trouble – it doesn't matter if it's a "spill", a "splash," a "droplet" or a "spray" – the result is the same.

Planning Security Operations Integration and Monitoring from the Beginning

The optimal time to involve information security is at the beginning. The earlier your security team can get into the development, architecture, planning and implementation phases, the better. This is called integration from origin (IFO). The pre-sales phase, during proof of value and proof of concept, is ideal because you'll be there to ask the tough questions (and validate the vendor's or provider's answers). Bring the results from your last tabletop exercise or security program assessment and ask a virtualization vendor or cloud provider how they would be handled. Ask what type of APIs the provider has to integrate their hosting server with a vulnerability scanner or an endpoint detection platform. Don't settle for an answer like "Yes, we have an API" — ask for API documentation that your security architecture or engineering teams can review. Integration and engagement should continue until you no longer have a relationship with the vendor or provider. Some (or all) of your security resources may need to be re-architected to interface directly with virtualization or cloud providers.

Unfortunately, most security operations teams find themselves inserted into the virtualization or cloud security loops much later than they should be. If your organization has deployed or is currently deploying cloud platforms and is already migrating applications, networks, endpoints, and resources, you will be coming in "in motion". The wrong time to design an airplane is when it's in the middle of flight. You want to avoid bolting your security resources onto an existing deployment. In larger or geographically distributed enterprises, you may be unpleasantly surprised to learn that your information technology department has already been in the virtualization and cloud world for quite a long time. That's probably not the case if you're a smaller to mid-sized organization and your security operations team is tightly integrated with the information technology team.

A typical scenario is that your operation detects, or is notified by another organization, that data has been found on various websites that appears to be from your company. Or you're provided with an IP address or set of addresses that have been communicating with C2 servers. After some investigation, you find out that the hosts involved with the incident map to endpoints hosted on a VMWare ESXi server or an Oracle Cloud Infrastructure deployment that you were unaware of. Not only is this a sad state of affairs but you'll discover cascading issues and questions. For instance, if your security team was unaware of a VMWare ESXi server hosting endpoints, there probably has been no other IS work on those endpoints, including vulnerability assessments and scans, operating system and application patching, and penetration testing.

Resources for Monitoring

Virtualization vendors and cloud providers are not new to integrating with IT and IS organizations. There are many resources available from all the major vendors and providers for monitoring and internal detection. Here are just a few examples that you can refer to when asking your vendor or provider what is available to help with your security operations monitoring mission:

- Amazon Macie for S3—This resource crawls through your S3 buckets and identifies where your most critical data is. Macie also employs machine learning to identify data access patterns that have been consistent in the past with attack patterns. (https://aws.amazon.com/macie/)
- Microsoft Azure SQL Threat Detection—This tool performs an automated review of your SQL access logs from sources that have been traditionally consistent with malicious behavior. Azure SQL database threat detection detects anomalous activities that may indicate unusual and potentially harmful attempts to access or exploit databases. (https://docs.microsoft.com/en-us/azure/sql-database/sql-database-threat-detection)
- Google Cloud Platform data leak prevention API—This API helps you better understand and manage sensitive data. It provides fast, scalable classification and redaction for sensitive data elements like credit card numbers, names, social security numbers, US and selected international identifier numbers, phone numbers and GCP credentials. (https://cloud.google.com/dlp/)

FireEye offers virtual environments for customers who want to shift from traditional physical appliance form factors. In FireEye VX or Cluster MVX deployments, network nodes deployed throughout your network still handle a majority of the static and signature-based detection activities. Objects are transported to analysis engines hosted in a cluster that is deployed locally to one or more of your data centers (or hosted in an Amazon data center). The deployment architecture looks like Figure 52:

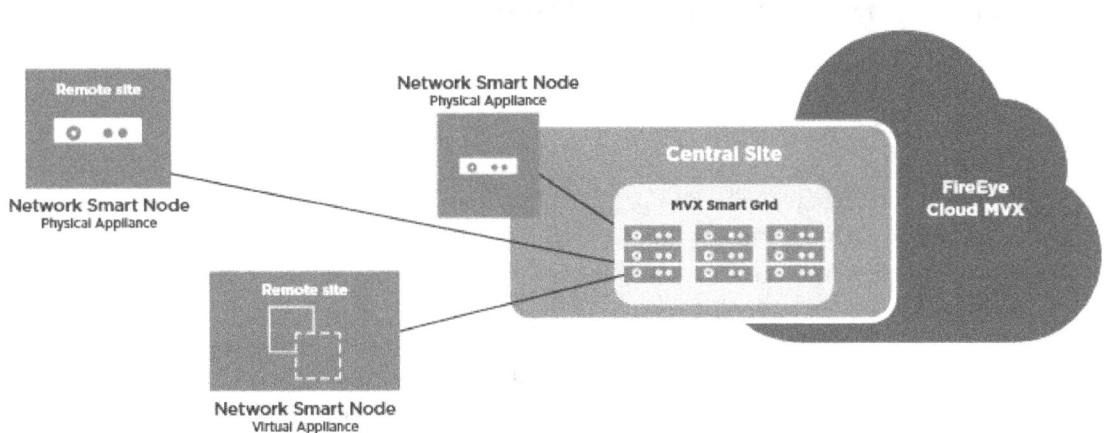

Figure 52: FireEye Smart Node and Cloud MVX deployment

Adjustment for the Team

Shifting from a physical, hands-on, analog world to a virtual-digital world is going to be a shock for some of your security operations team. Your tier 1 triage and smoke-fire jumpers won't have this issue; nor will most levels of cyber security analysts, because they've been living in it with packets, logs, alerts, events, alarms, memory or hard drive images, and so on. It's your firewall admins, your intrusion detection-protection administrators, your solutions architects and information security support or engineering staff. If they're not experienced with each specific cloud provider, they're in for multiple, steep learning curves.

Questions to Ask About Cloud Resources

Here are 16 questions regarding incident response and handling when resources are no longer physical:

1. How will you engage in live response, such as memory or disk image acquisition on a virtual resource hosted in the cloud?

2. Who owns the VMs? If the provider owns them, how will you take full disk images or memory images for endpoints hosted in the cloud?"

3. What are the costs and limitations on pulling data out of the cloud, rather than accessing data within the cloud? Some organizations plan to put agents on their cloud-deployed endpoints and proxy that data out of the cloud and over to their physical endpoint detection and protection appliances. This may be costly or impossible.

4. How is data encryption handled on your cloud endpoints? If you have to do a file acquisition on a cloud-managed, cloud-encrypted virtual machine, who owns the encryption keys?

5. Who is responsible for monitoring cloud scalability? Most clouds support an auto-scaling feature that works well for legitimate uses. If a malicious process chews up your resources, your cloud infrastructure may be dynamically growing (while you're being charged for it). Coin miners such as BitCoin are notorious resource hogs.

6. How will you perform vulnerability assessments? Are your current resources capable of scanning an AWS S3 bucket or a Microsoft Azure VPC?

7. Does your cloud provider allow you to scan or sweep all networks and endpoints at one time for a set of IOCs? Some cloud providers may not allow some forms of sweeping and scanning for performance or load-balancing reasons. Your cloud provider's architecture may have groups, clusters or containers of endpoints utilizing a shared storage area network or network-attached storage device. Scans and sweeps in those environments tend to not work well with shared hardware resources.

8. If a critical breach occurs, how do you quarantine or contain virtual systems? This has two parts. You need to stop access by external resources through the front door, and you need access to the quarantined system through the back door.

9. If you are in a heavily regulated industry or require yearly or semi-annual certification and accreditation, do you have the ability to conduct the required blue team, red team, penetration testing or physical onsite inspections of the cloud provider's data centers?

10. The cloud provider wants to shut down access to a virtual machine, network or cluster due to an intrusion, but your threat and intelligence team has recommended "monitor and do not block." How would that conflict be resolved?

11. For asset tracking and inventory management, how are new deployments of machines, endpoints or networks discovered and reported to the security operations team?

12. In a disaster and recovery scenario, where will your backups go—to another cloud-based system or back into the internal network? This affects your organization's ability to maintain availability, one leg of the CIA triad.

13. Does the data center reside in your country or another country? There may be particular legal or regulatory issues and requirements.

14. Does the cloud provider supply their own IT support, do they send it offshore, or do they outsource to a third party? Offshoring or having IT support handled in countries that are known to engage in corporate or economic espionage is dangerous. Is your cloud provider willing to state, in writing, that they will not use offshore support for your systems?

15. What vendor's physical hardware is being used? Is your cloud provider willing to say? If you are working with government or military customers, partners, or suppliers, they may want an assurance that their data is not on a lower-cost platform that is sourced from countries known for corporate or economic espionage.

16. Is there a written agreement about who is liable should the cloud provider's infrastructure or internal resources be compromised? How much threat and intel will the provider share about compromises, including those that may not have directly impacted your cloud deployments? This may not seem like a big deal, but one bad apple can spoil the whole bunch.

Questions to Ask About Penetration Testing and Vulnerability Assessment

If your internal blue teams and red teams (penetration testers) were busy before your organization went virtual, business is about to pick up. At least, theoretically. Your penetration testing teams need to adjust to the greater pacing challenges that often come with virtualization and cloud providers. So will your vulnerability assessment, scanning and management team, as well as your inline network security detection and protection resources, your anti-virus/anti-malware resources, and so on. You must validate policies and controls that affect essential pen testing or vulnerability assessment missions. Here are some questions to ask:

1. Are you allowed to perform blue team and red team pen testing into the virtual environment and cloud platforms? Is this documented in service-level agreements or terms of service? If pen testing is allowed, what is considered in or out of scope?

2. Does the cloud provider already have a penetration testing team? If so, how do you synchronize missions so your internal team and the provider's team don't accidentally stomp on each other?

3. Are only the required ports open and accessible to the outside world?

4. Are only the required protocols and services passed through the cloud?

5. How are credentials secured?

6. Are your internal infrastructure details (IP addresses, hostnames, network routing paths, and so on) protected from external access?
7. Are encryption keys secured? Not only keys to operating systems and data but also SSL keys used by agents, applications, information technology or security apps.
8. Does encryption function successfully through external access and internal access? Who owns the encryption keys?
9. For agent-based functionality, are agent SSL/TLS or PKI certificates backed up? This is critical. If a virtual endpoint or a group of virtual machines must be terminated and dynamically replaced, what is the process for backing up older SS/TLS or PKI certificates and reimporting to the new virtual machines? Loss of certificates can prevent agents from ever connecting back to their server resources. Not a problem if you have a few endpoints, but if this happens on the scale of thousands or tens of thousands of endpoints, your security operations team is in for some long weeks.
10. Are privileges assigned properly?
11. Are configuration changes logged, monitored and reviewed appropriately?
12. Can rogue or unauthorized processes dynamically alter a virtualization environment?
13. Will you know when machine instances or Virtual PCs are revised, dynamically deployed or decommissioned/terminated? How will you be informed?
14. If a process locks up so badly that a manual reboot of the virtual PC or machine instance is required, how quickly can the system administrators or cloud provider support staff locate virtual machine and do the equivalent of a manual power cycle?

Scenario: A Rocky Transition from Physical to Virtual/Cloud

The shift to the cloud is not as easy as copyinga physical deployment to a virtual environment. In addition to the lists of questions and issues discussed earlier, other issues will come up that you might not have planned for. The following scenario is all too typical.

1. A mid-sized company's online training product has become so popular (and profitable) that it constantly requires additional infrastructure. The company decides to migrate the product and supporting applications from their physical data centers to a cloud provider called BigBiz's Happy Cloud. Initially, 24 virtual servers are deployed and time is allowed for migration, transition and burn-in time. As demand grows and requirements increase, BigBiz's Happy Cloud cluster settings scale dynamically as needed. Everything is going well for several months.
2. Between a Tuesday and the following Friday, the virtual server count increases from 24 systems to 38 and then to 64. The IS team notes the unusual increase, but it does not seem to be an urgent issue and the manager plans to investigate it on Monday. On Friday evening, an FBI special investigative agent visits the company:

company servers have been detecting communications to known malicious command and control servers hosted in Pakistan.

3. By the next morning, initial analysis shows that all 64 servers are experiencing heavy CPU utilization tied to a process called miner-patch.exe, which is stored in C:\Program Files\SQL. The file is acquired from a few servers and the company's dynamic analysis resource identifies the object as malicious and classifies it as a BitMiner application. As the BitMiner ran wild, the cloud provider did exactly what it was configured to do and scaled automatically.

4. All 24 original virtual machines are rolled back to a known good operational state. The other virtual machines are quickly de-commissioned and terminated. By Monday morning, the incident is cleaned up, all traces of minor-patch.exe and associated files have been removed, the SQL vulnerability has been patched, and the company has blocked access to the C2 servers entirely.

Everything is back to normal and no customers were affected, so all is well, isn't it? Let's continue the scenario:

5. The hackers—who originally were just looking for a few systems to own (pwn) in order to grow their BitMining operations—are frustrated. They decide to get revenge by locking up the online training company's servers, whose IP ranges they know. After setting up some virtual machines through a shady virtualization hosting provider, and using TOR for anonymity, the hackers use a THC-Hydra variant called HydraGTK to create havoc. The attack application looks like Figure 53:

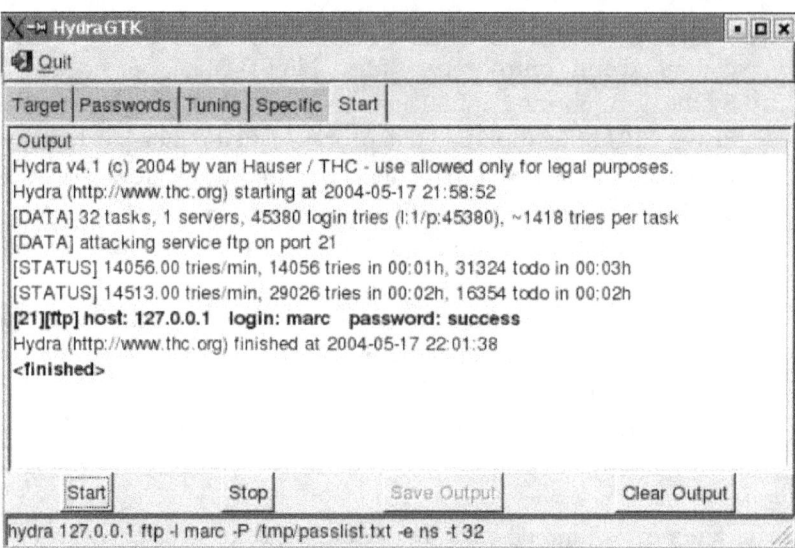

Figure 53: HydraGTK attack

They also use the Low Orbit Ion Cannon to throw so much junk at the servers that they slow down or simply stop servicing customers.

6. A week after the prior incident was closed, server administrators report that they can no longer log in remotely to any of the servers. Local InfoSec analysts using privileged accounts are also locked out. The customer support phones are flooded with complaints from customers who can't reach the servers. All remote accounts are persistently locked out and the network interfaces bound to the web server applications are terminally saturated. The company is under a DDoS attack.

7. The company has a subscription to a DDoS protection product, but it turns out that the subscription was canceled four months ago because "it hadn't been used in five years." The only way to recover the machines is to log in to a physical device via a crash cart with a direct keyboard connection into a console. The company asks the cloud provider to do this.

8. The cloud provider reports that the online training company's 24 virtual servers are spread throughout four different data centers—two in the US, two in Europe. Although the cloud provider knows the general geographic location of the customer's resources, they can't pinpoint exact physical location details, due to the scale and breadth of BigBiz's Happy Cloud data centers. Locating and cleaning up all 24 servers will take at least four or five hours. Until then, the online product is unavailable. Did I mention that this product is one of the company's major revenue streams?

What were the big mistakes here?

- A rogue or unknown process was introduced into the environment, but no immediate, actionable alerts were created. There was no way to distinguish abnormal from normal activity.

- Auto-scaling with the cloud provider's dynamic configuration change happened without any review. Infrastructure change notifications that required human validation would have revealed the context of the changes.

- The online training company didn't have the proper experience or skills to engage in cloud migration. Migrating a critical, revenue-generating company application to a cloud platform without doing due diligence and tabletop exercises could be considered negligent. The company should have sought provider assistance or third-party consulting services.

- The existing dynamic analysis solution wasn't placed inline with network traffic. Files had to be acquired and submitted for analysis manually. If the victim company had deployed an inline, web-based object analyzer, it could have detected miner-patch.exe (or its dropper/payload files) "in transit", providing a heads-up to the security team of a malicious file on the move.

- There was no monitoring or identification of C2 activity. An inline network monitoring device that knew malicious destination IPs could have at least detected outbound connectivity tied back to miner-patch.exe. If the in-line network device was configured to block, the C2 callbacks could have been blocked in real time.

- Responsibility for asset discovery and mapping infrastructure virtual to physical location was not explicitly assigned; therefore, no one was responsible. While it could be argued that the cloud provider should be able to pinpoint a server's physical location quickly, if they can't, the customer/subscriber should. If this were a ransomware campaign that was rapidly spreading via an advanced distribution exploit kit or laterally moving mechanism, four or five hours would be more than enough to cause massive pain and loss of resources.

Attackers, whether or not they are targeting a specific a victim, are adapting to hacking in the cloud. Even if these hackers didn't initially target the online training company, they more than likely noticed their BitMining infrastructure growing rapidly and dynamically, reflecting a cloud provider. Our incident response and handling—our entire security operations infrastructure and program—needs to be able to adapt and evolve as rapidly as virtualization and cloud are growing and evolving.

Fusing Security Resources Directly to Cloud Infrastructure

Both virtualization and the cloud can be agile and self-scaling, requiring little to no effort to deploy an infrastructure and direct interaction through APIs and remote calls. The traditional firewalls, IDS, anti-virus, anti-malware, endpoint detection resources, and so on aren't typically associated with adjectives like *agile* or *self-scaling*.

When it comes to virtualization and cloud, we can no longer rely on a human to notify another human, to manually start and stop processes, and so on. Our asymmetric operations have many points of failures, opportunities for drops, and long waiting times when someone is out of town or on vacation. They are no longer able to keep pace with the volume and velocity of workloads created by modern virtualization environments and cloud platforms. We've got to mature from an asymmetric, analog, piece-by-piece workflow and infrastructure to a symmetric, digital, system-to-system fusing between our security operations and virtualization and cloud resources. This is more than just "machine-to-machine" integration; we're trying to wire hundreds of machines to hundreds of other machines. Scaling on this order requires system-to-system interaction and platform-to-platform integration.

It wouldn't be hard to spin up 100 AWS machine instances to support a multi-petabyte machine learning data store for a massive data training and modeling project to tune machine learning algorithms. Through the AWS S3 APIs, signals can be sent to an asset tracking system that is leveraged by the security operations team. From there, a security orchestration platform can run the logic processing required to determine that those new machines just received a CentOS 7 operating system image, which was subsequently updated with current patches. Before applications are layered in, a vulnerability scan can engage automatically and send results directly to a vulnerability analyst.

That would only be the start of a long set of courses of actions or playbooks that could run from cloud-created virtual machines to layering in operating systems and applications, running multiple vulnerability assessments, baking in security endpoints or automatically deploying network sensor nodes tied back to larger detection capabilities. If one of those CentOS 7 virtual machines becomes compromised or is involved in a security incident detected by an endpoint security agent, orchestration can automatically move that system to a "dirty VLAN", limiting its exposure to other healthy virtual machines in the cluster. Parallel courses of action can engage in more levels of automation, such as leveraging a netstat or "network details" acquisition/live response script, transporting output from the SOAR API to APIs at sites like URLVoid or IPVoid, and collecting results for analyst assessment. While all that is running, there can be a human intervention point where an analyst can approve the continued containment or take an alternate course of action.

Clouds You're Already In That Require Revised Processes

Your organization is probably working with cloud platforms already, such as

- SalesForce
- Office 365
- Dropbox (and many other variants)
- Okta
- Duo
- LinkedIn
- TripIt
- DocuSign

While you've probably had mostly successful and smooth relationships with cloud-hosted applications and platforms, you need established plans, run books, playbooks, points of contacts established with specific security teams at your cloud service and application providers. Anything that you think might become a problem during an incident, intrusion, breach or compromise should be well thought out before any of those happen.

Suppose you had a SalesForce account that seemed to be navigating into hundreds or thousands of customer records, downloading an abnormally large amount of data from each customer record. That account was recently placed on a watch list because the owner has given notice that they are departing from the company in two weeks. What are your incident response processes?

- Do you have methods of detecting and being alerted about that type of abnormal activity?
- Is SalesForce directly connected or fused with your security operations team?
- Along with alerts that should be generated, are access logs being captured for later analysis?
- Is there an ability in near real time to start engaging in endpoint recording activity, like where all that data is being downloaded or saved to and how it is moving through the endpoint and network?
- Would your interaction with SalesForce be proactive in this scenario or reactive?

Similarly, you need incident response processes if you are notified about accidental uploads through Dropbox that contained company confidential or proprietary information.

In the hack of the US Democratic National Convention in 2016, Microsoft OneDrive accounts were used as a vector for exfiltrating data out of compromised American organizations involved with the convention and associated with political targets. According to Microsoft documentation for OneDrive, endpoints require access to a number of fully qualified domain names through two ports, TCP 80 and 443. They connect over TCP port 80 for system access and use port 443 for passing credentials and ongoing communication. While this was a risky move, I suspect the threat actor decided that the probability of HTTPS interception and secure communications monitoring was low enough to make the risk acceptable. Even so, it's still possible to do detection on TCP and IP headers. Those will never be encrypted because the packets must be routed. While detection visibility to packet payload was probably a no-go, the risk is about what can be detected via packet headers. A process as easy as assessing TCP and IP header and NetFlow data, monitoring connections, and monitoring the size and frequency of packets connecting outbound to a foreign server is enough to tell you that something abnormal is going on. The challenge is that not many organizations can spend the time or resources in contemplating all the alternative vectors a threat actor could use exfiltrate data. Even if they did, it's a never-ending chess game.

This business is heavily risk oriented. What is the acceptable risk your organization is willing to assume? For me, those decisions are way above my pay grade. I don't mind advising anyone on the positive and negative aspect of decisions or making recommendations on how to evaluate, assess, observe or even measure risk. However, the decision about what level of risk is acceptable is typically in the purview of a chief risk officer or a chief information security officer. In the US Army, that decision is made no lower than a one-star Brigadier General. At the end of the day, security is about risk levels and control—and whether the benefits of virtualization are worth the risk of giving up some control.

Chapter 10: Agents and Inline Devices

Oh! the tangled web we weave when we strive for complete security functionality.

Most seasoned sysadmins will roll their eyes when they hear, "We just purchased product X and we need to deploy a new agent to our entire endpoint fleet". Every agent adds another layer of delay to power cycles and reboots. Some agents just don't play well together. When agents conflict or get it wrong, they can spin out in a tremendous outburst, including lockups and the dreaded Windows "blue screen of death". In Linux and UNIX, agents have caused epic kernel panics and system halts.

The problem escalates with servers. Should an endpoint agent on a laptop or desktop fail, it brings down a single system. Should an endpoint agent on a server, switch, router or storage device fail, it can take out services and resources for hundreds or thousands of users. It's a dilemma because without direct functionality components at the endpoint, we just can't effectively measure, collect, capture or control some things. Getting a memory image, interrogating services, collecting network stats like local and remote IP connections and port activity all require hooks directly on the endpoint. Some vendors have tried "agentless" efforts that haven't turned out well.

On the networking side, security architecture has become so complicated, with multiple junctures of inline networking devices, that the path from A to B is no longer a straight shot. Inline devices for intrusion detection, platforms for static or dynamic analysis, full packet capture devices, proxy devices, firewall devices, network security monitor ingress and egress points (such as Bro, Suricata, and Security Onion) can be deployed. Then layer in non-security performance and measurement resources like NetFlow, latency and transport measurement devices, load balancers, virtual private network appliances, traffic aggregators, and wide area network transmission devices. A failure or disruption by any of these devices can cause pain.

Multiple Agents and Inline Devices

The problem of excessive layers of agents on every endpoint in the enterprise is also known as excessive agent syndrome, agent saturation or bloat, agent overload, connector complexity, and by many other names. Figure 54 shows an example of multiple information security agents:

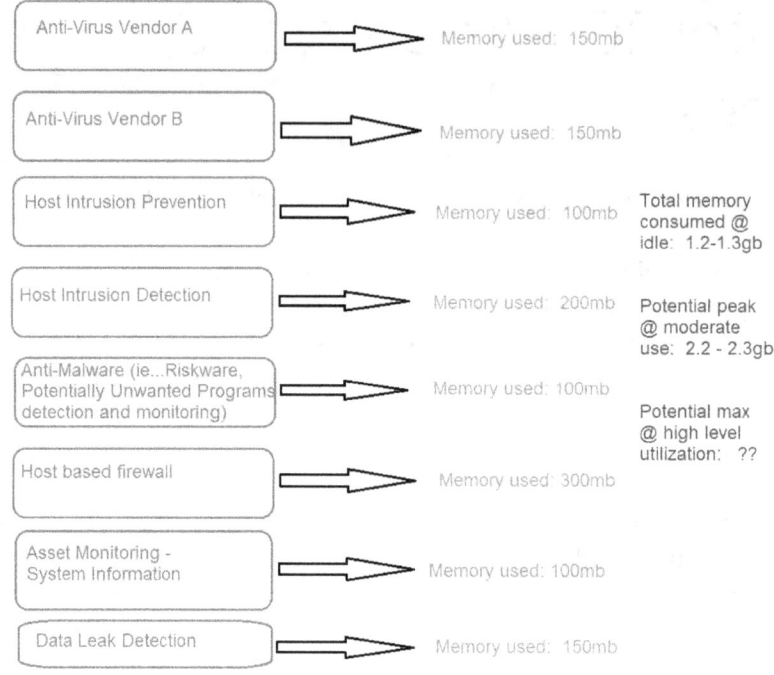

Figure 54: Layers of agents

It's not uncommon to use two anti-virus products, especially if there have been incidents where one vendor detected a threat and the other didn't. For example, perhaps the endpoint is covered by a regulation or certification and accreditation package that requires vendor A's anti-virus to be deployed. If the regional or local security team prefers vendor B's product, they'll deploy both. Some organizations use multiple A/V products to spot-check each other or provide weightings when alerts fire.

If a laptop or desktop has 4 gigabytes (GB) of memory, even a moderate load consumes over 50% of the system's resources. Many enterprise environments have simply become oversaturated.

We've compounded the agent bloating issue by layering in inline network devices or capture hogs that can create the following problems:

- Multiple failure points
- Duplication of packet storage
- Distortion of alerts (when vendors parse and evaluate conditions differently, creating different levels of alerts)
- Disruption and latency
- Multiple points where state changes can impact dynamic routing protocols

- Multiple devices that can create "dirty network" points or chew up packets incorrectly. Examples include:
    - Duplicate packets, loss of synchronous traffic down to asynchronous traffic
    - Session splitting or packet loss
    - Device oversaturation caused by incorrect scaling, resulting in intermittent changes to bypass mode

These conditions can range from minor annoyances when the device is deployed in a TAP or SPAN mode all the way to major disruption or packet flow stoppage when the device is in inline blocking mode with failover set to fail-closed mode. Always validate what conditions will cause an inline device to go into bypass mode.

Note: Double-check your vendor's definition for fail-open and fail-closed modes when you configure active blocking. For FireEye devices, fail-open means the devices continue passing packets and the network connection is considered open. Fail-closed means the connection is closed and the devices do not pass any packets.

Figure 55 shows where various inline devices have been introduced to enterprise-level security architecture:

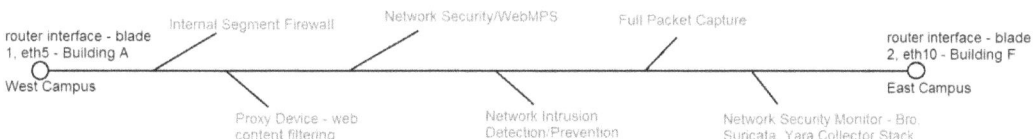

Figure 55: Multiple inline devices

This is an extremely simplified diagram that only encompasses one segment of a network. You won't just have one firewall, proxy device, network IDS or IPS, packet capture device—you'll have a fleet of each.

Unicorn Agents and Special Snowflakes

Network and security architects and system administrators have heard this one before: "Our agent is required to run this program" or "My agent is unique". Here is the problem with multiple unicorn agents or special snowflake devices – when everything is special and unique, from a higher-level perspective, *nothing* is special. An enterprise security operations team can be dealing with more than 30 different resources and may have 10-15 agents, connectors, and collectors deployed to every endpoint in an organization's fleet of desktops, laptops, servers, tablets, and cell phones. Any one agent on an endpoint may be happy and content, running normally, always available and 100% functional. Yet almost none were designed to integrate together or to work in the presence of the others. Technical problems can pop up at the most inopportune times (such as 2:00 on a Monday morning while end-of-quarter financial closing is processing on multiple servers across the globe, all of which have the same troublesome agents deployed).

Common Issues with Multiple Agents

Whether they are called agents, collectors, connectors, or distributors, all agents have issues from time to time. Before you decide to deploy an agent across your environment, you should check the track record of the vendor and plan a phased rollout.

Unfortunately, when agents fail, their failures are burned in the minds of administrators, security operations teams and management around the world. Some of those snafus will be remembered long after the malware is gone or the incident has been forgotten. Here are some agent issues that have given agents bad names:

- Memory leaks
- Race conditions with other agents
- Resource contention with other agents
- Garbage collection disruption or cleanup issues that cause bloating
- Non-discretionary handling of data (passing data collected from the operating systems and applications, through the agents, up to a server, out to the cloud and then to who knows where)
- Non-responsiveness that requires an administrator to intervene, causing premature stops or restarts
- Distortion caused by agent actions (for example, an agent copies an object to a quarantined or isolated location and then deletes the original object, thus changing timestamps essential to a forensics case or incident timeline analysis)
- Multiple sessions created when agents lock objects (an attempt to unlock an object results in an error and leaves the object locked with multiple open or half-open sessions, exhausting resources and preventing other applications from using the same object)

Agent Tampering

Users and administrators have had so many problems with agent-based security resources that instead of properly running them to ground or performing root cause analysis, their first reaction is to stop or uninstall the agent. This has become so prevalent that many modern agents now have agent tampering protection features. Many installers support command-line switches applied during installation that allow you to require an uninstall password. In Microsoft environments, if .msi (Microsoft Installer) files are used, you can couple them with the Microsoft Executive Windows Installer application – msiexec.exe. The FireEye Endpoint Security Agents now handle this through an uninstall password that is defined at the HX primary controller as a configuration option called "Removal Protection", as seen in Figure 56 (currently only available to Windows agents 26 and higher):

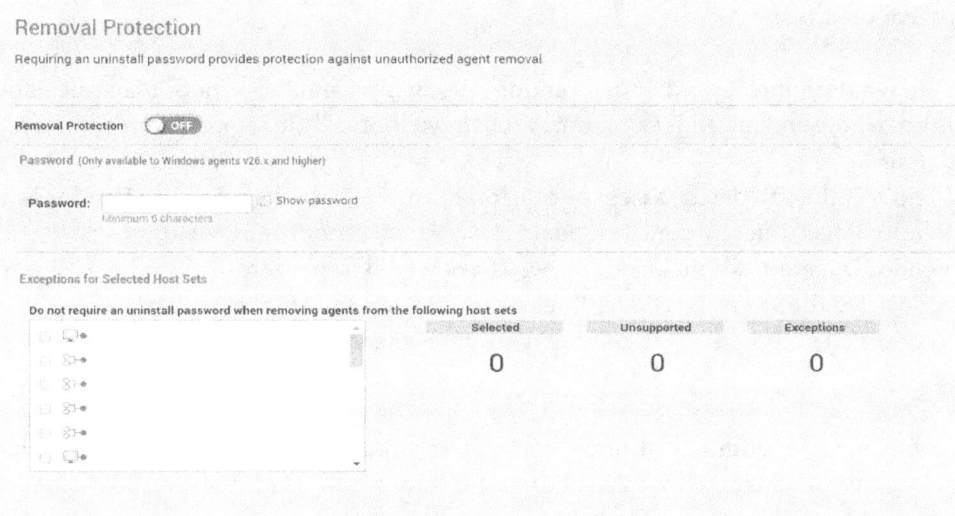

Figure 56: Setting an uninstall password

With other products or external scripting, it's possible to setup a watchdog process. If something happens with the endpoint agent, a watchdog process can restart or spawn a new agent process. It's also possible to leverage automation and orchestration to automatically restart killed or stopped endpoint agents.

Agent tampering and unwanted uninstallations aren't limited to frustrated users or system administrators. Hackers, intruders, and threat actors typically engage in two activities during the initial reconnaissance and compromise phases of an incident. First, they recon the environment to determine what security resources are active and running. This can be as simple as running a tasklist or tasklist/v on a Microsoft Windows endpoint or a ps -ef or top on a Linux/Unix/Mac endpoint. Next, they stop, disable or uninstall those security resources. (A skilled threat actor might skip this step if they are confident they can evade security resources or simply live off the land and do nothing that would match a malicious signature, definition, or IOC.)

Alert and Event Conflicts—When Analysts Must Become Digital Interpreters

With multiple agents, connectors, and collectors creating issues on the front end (the endpoint) and multiple inline devices creating issues on the back end, there is a high probability of conflict between alerts and events from different vendors. Most vendors' products don't integrate well with each other and can vary in accuracy, efficacy and relevance. They don't even define events the same way. For example:

- Different terminology: what one vendor calls an alert another vendor may call an event. A third vendor might call it an alarm. A fourth vendor calls it a notification and merely writes details to a log.
- Vendor A doesn't detect, assess or categorize an object the same way as Vendor B.
- Vendor B has different content update cycles from Vendor A or Vendor C.
- Vendor D identifies a malicious object as a new, unknown zero-day exploit, while Vendor A detected the same object over three years ago and called it something else.
- Vendors all detect an object, but each attributes the object to a different attacker or threat group.

Instead of looking at individual platforms, you may rely on a third-party solution to pull it all together. However, as alerts move from one vendor through an API, SYSLOG, RSYSLOG or CEF into another vendor's product, a lot can get lost in translation.

An alert starts with a high level of fidelity, such as this from a FireEye Network Security smart node (Figure 57):

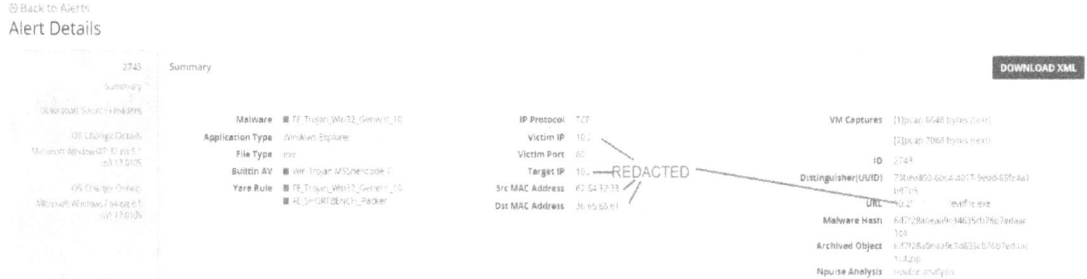

Figure 57: Alert details on a smart node

After being transported through the node, exported through a CEF processor or SMTP sender, ingested by a third-party vendor, parsed and potentially altered to fit the vendor's schema or taxonomy, and rendered for display, it might look completely different.

Infosec and cyber security professionals should not be required to spend valuable time and cycles interpreting conflicting information or translating versions of an original alert. They can end up so confused they don't know what to do next or which vendor's information to roll with. We covered in an earlier chapter the way such conditions can lead to analyst paralysis. It's a common state to be in these days. Security architectures layered on top of one another become a conglomeration of detection grids, sensor groups, protection resources, packet captures, multiple resources and a dizzying array of information overload. Some companies have made their products, platforms and services so complex and tangled, I don't even know where you would start with something like Figure 58:

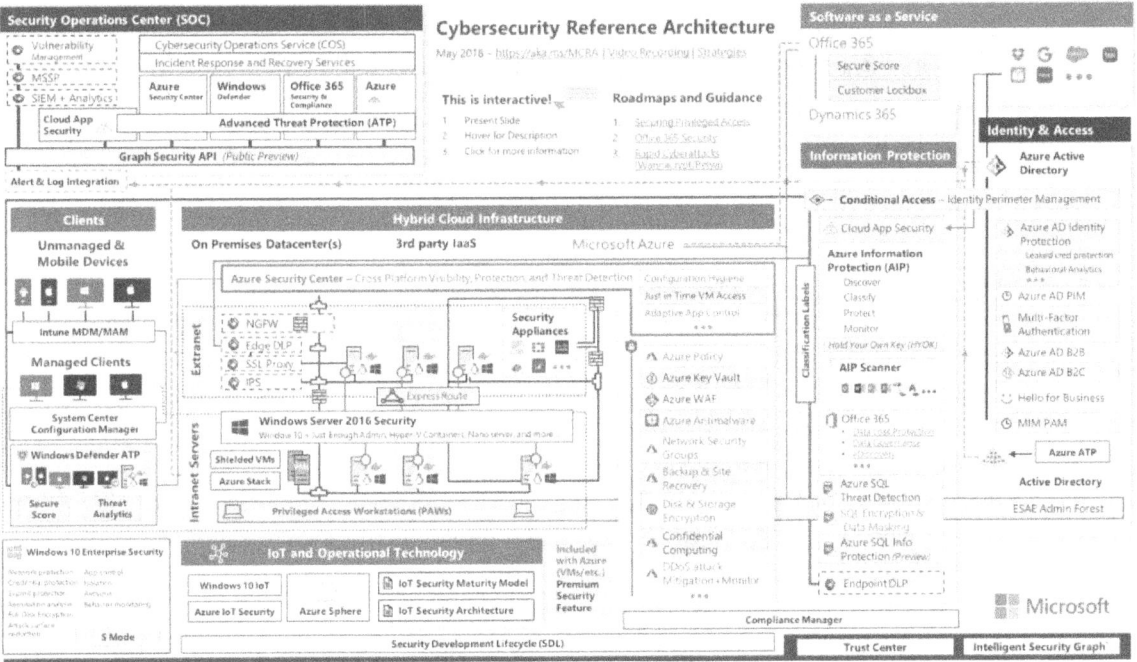

Figure 58: Complicated product UI reflects poor integration

Reference: https://cloudblogs.microsoft.com/microsoftsecure/2018/06/06/cybersecurity-reference-architecture-security-for-a-hybrid-enterprise/

Although it probably makes sense to security engineers at Microsoft, this collage of acronyms, product names, operating systems, enterprise solutions, back-end resources like SQL and Active Directory and so on is so complicated that all it seems to say is, "Look at all the things we can do!"

I don't fault Microsoft for that jumbled diagram. Security operations, integration across multiple systems and coverage in as many areas as possible for detection, defense and protection aren't easy.

However, what does everything in the diagram do for Apple operating systems and applications? Or for Google apps, the Chrome browser or the Android operating system? How does it cover Linux operating systems, open-source applications or mobile devices like tablets and cell phones that don't run Windows Surface? How does it address attackers who don't use malware?

Agent Unification and Inline Resource Consolidation

What can we do to start realigning our security operations practices into a more streamlined, cohesive and integrated set of resources that enable our teams and professionals to get the right amount of information (no more, no less), at the right time, in front of the right eyes to do the right job?

It starts with narrowing down your choice of platform providers. Look for the best one that offers or is pursuing the following:

- Scope and range of products and multiple platforms that integrate with each other
- A model of agent unification or common agent architecture, as well as user interface standardization across its portfolio
- Innovation driven by a wide range of field-based, hands-on practitioners that not only work in the same range as your security teams but use the same platforms, products and services they recommend to their customers.
- Form factors that match your deployment scenarios: physical appliances, cloud platforms or a hybrid; virtual and ISO formats for smaller deployments such as satellite or regional offices, labs, training environments.

At FireEye, we continually improve our own platforms in multiple areas. Our Endpoint Security agents are now multi-layered and resemble Figure 59:

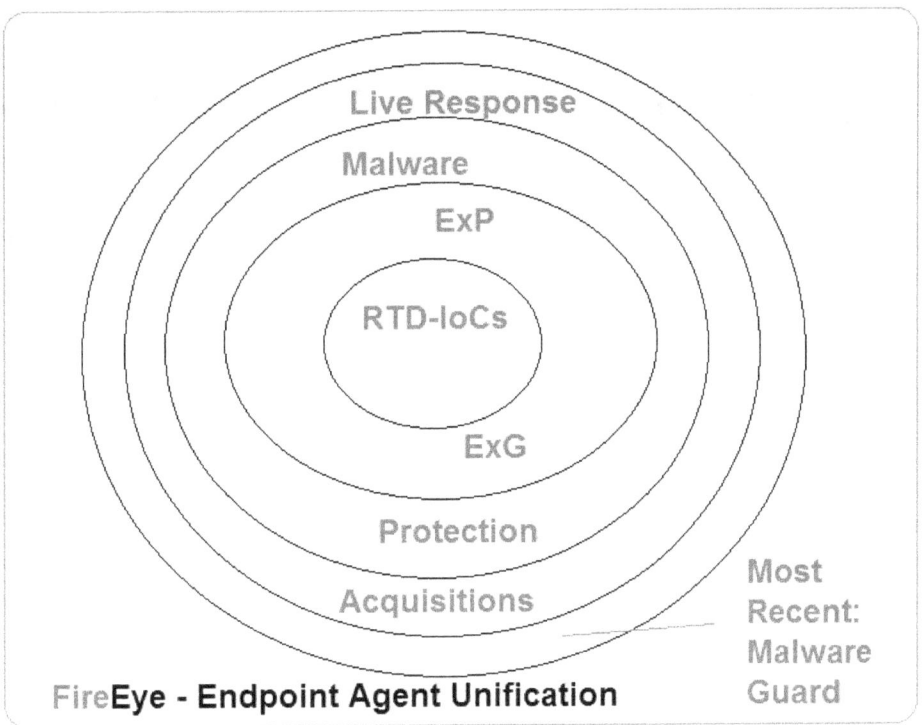

Figure 59: FireEye endpoint agent unification

At the core of our endpoint agents are:

- RTD-IOCs—Real-time detection with indicators of compromise (also called rules)

As an additional layer of detection and functionality, we have:

- Exploit Guard (ExG)—Detects exploits run from applications, browsers and operating systems components in memory
- Exploit Prevention (ExP)—Allows you to prevent suspicious behaviors, terminate an exploited process, and notify the user when an exploit has been blocked
- Malware Protection—Anti-virus replacement
- Malware Guard—Machine-learning-trained signatureless detection
- Live response/scripted data acquisitions

Instead of multiple physical appliances that introduce multiple points of packet capture throughout your enterprise, FireEye offers a consolidated model of deployment that captures packets once (see Figure 52 in Chapter 9).

When Agents Collide: Whitelisting and Modular Troubleshooting

This book contains very little troubleshooting because there is far too much to cover, but here are a few basic techniques for troubleshooting agents.

If anti-virus agent A quarantines a DLL or EXE associated with agent B when feature X is run, there isn't necessarily a problem with either agent. A conflict is the more probable cause. Many agents, including FireEye agents, engage in activities that resemble suspicious behavior to other security-oriented agents. An xAgt.exe file acquiring files from multiple endpoints could be considered suspicious. An agent executing a live response/scripted data acquisition to list eight levels of files and folders and collect 100 registry keys associated with malware can also be look suspicious to other agents. Without context, agents have no idea whether what they are assessing is the result of another agent or the result of a malicious process.

The first thing I suggest is whitelisting the files driving FireEye agents with third-party security products. Likewise, get a list of essential files and folders of your third-party security products and whitelist them with the FireEye Endpoint Security (HX) platform.

If whitelisting between multiple security agents/products doesn't resolve technical conflicts, deeper troubleshooting is required. Modular troubleshooting is essentially disabling all parts of an agent and re-enabling one module at a time, across a narrow group of systems, in order to isolate the feature that needs deeper investigation. Most of the functions of our agents, including Real-Time Detection, Exploit Guard and Malware Guard, can be configured at a global level and can be disabled at a host-set level. From there, the list of troubleshooting routes and alternatives is long. FireEye offers troubleshooting resources that range from customer support to troubleshooting training courses. FireEye also has community forums, Designated Support Engineers (DSEs), and a dedicated group writing technical documentation that is available via docs.fireeye.com.

Secure, Linux-Like Mainstream Operating Systems?

While I don't think we'll see this anytime soon, there have been industry talks about creating more secure mainstream operating systems. In many ways, agents are required to supplement the security weaknesses of operating systems and applications regarding commercial and enterprise-level information security. In order to obtain the required level of flexibility, visibility, measurement, detection and protection, operating systems and applications need to be extended beyond what is available "out of the box". If those features were designed to reach the level of security that commercial businesses and enterprises require, the need for multiple or heavy agents would be reduced. There have been many discussions about having desktop or laptop mainstream operating systems adopt a model similar to those used by organizations like https://www.qubes-os.org/ or http://www.trustedbsd.org/ Such a model enhances integrated ability to build in what we now do with agents, and allows third-party vendors to directly hook into the operating system.

Chapter 11: Actionable Cyber Threat Intelligence

An old cowboy once said to a young whippersnapper: "Don't shoot the target where it was--shoot it where it's going."

This is a popular phrase in the military and in sports, and it's just as applicable to cyber threat and intelligence. Your cyber threat and intelligence (CTI) should primarily focus on where it needs to be in the future. This chapter explains how to get the most from the CTI objects that you collect. When we refer to objects in this chapter, we mean *indicators of compromise, signatures, definitions, rulesets,* and *artifacts.* Tactical CTI refers to objects that you can use across detection, defensive and protection platforms, grids or systems. To be useful, CTI objects must be *usable, actionable, effective,* and *relevant.*

Tactical CTI

Many customers and organizations that I have observed have a CTI program or capability that ends up being a massive reporting engine. Often, the entire purpose of the CTI group is to produce lengthy intelligence reports or briefings for internal organizations. There is certainly a place for the big dossiers on threat actor groups, tactics, techniques, motivations, potential hypothesis on attribution, and so on at a *strategic* level. On a *tactical* level, however, firewalls, SIEMs, IDS, IPS, proxies, and so on can't ingest reports or briefings.

CTI programs must be atomic—meaningful at the object level. They must be usable, deployable, effective, actionable and most of all, relevant. If it's not relevant to your organization, it's a waste of your resources.

Defining Intel Requirements

Threat intelligence programs must start with two questions:

- What are our intelligence requirements (IR), and how can we define them?
- What are our Priority Intel Requirements (PIR)—the things we should work on first?

Some organizations start their cyber threat and intel programs by subscribing to as many threat and intelligence feeds as possible and pumping out reports to a distribution list, without defining their requirements. If they don't know what they want to accomplish, they are just blindly throwing darts towards a wall.

All threat and intelligence work should start with defining your IR and PIR, then developing a program based on those requirements. Your IR and PIR drive the data you'll need for defining the types of indicators, signatures, definitions, correlation rules, rulesets and artifacts to collect, curate, synthesize, distribute and manage. They also determine what context should be associated with those objects. Your IR and PIR also shouldn't remain static. Regular review of those requirements is essential, measuring how successful (or unsuccessful) your CTI work was, and redefining them as needed. A good cadence to start with is an intelligence requirement review once a quarter and then adjust as needed.

Where CTI Programs Typically Fail

We can define at least six reasons that attempts to do something meaningful with all your threat intel typically fail.

Data Without Context

I've read and dare say I've even created data that I thought was essential to distribute without defining why it was important and how it was relevant to the organization. Cyber threat and intel, whether created or consumed, needs context and requires organizational meaning. Without it, that data creates noise and noise must be filtered or ignored, or else it becomes an obstruction. Here is an example of data or indicators without meaning. Imagine receiving a list like this with instructions, "Notify us if you get alerts correlated to activity with the following MD5s":

```
001dd76872d80801692ff942308c64e6
002325a0a67fded0381b5648d7fe9b8e
00dbb9e1c09dbdafb360f3163ba5a3de
00f24328b282b28bc39960d55603e380
0115338e11f85d7a2226933712acaae8
0141955eb5b90ce25b506757ce151275
0149b7bd7218aab4e257d28469fddb0d
016da6ee744b16656a2ba3107c7a4a29
01e0dc079d4e33d8edd050c4900818da
024fd07dbdacc7da227bede3449c2b6a
0285bd1fbdd70fd5165260a490564ac8
02a2d148faba3b6310e7ba81eb62739d
02c65973b6018f5d473d701b3e7508b2
034374db2d35cf9da6558f54cec8a455
03ae71eba61af2d497e226da3954f3af
0469a42d71b4a55118b9579c8c772bb6
```

Without context about what they are or how they relate to your intelligence or priority intel requirements, that list of MD5s is meaningless to you. A higher-up threat and intel provider or a third-party organization may not be able to give you the context for various reasons (it's classified, it's part of an ongoing investigation, there's a risk of burning a source or tipping off a threat actor, and so on). Sometimes the explanation is as narrow as "Because my boss told me to do this". However, I would strongly demand more details and if they can't be provided, they I'd be hesitant to do anything with this list because to my organization, it's nothing more than noise without context.

Indicators, Signatures, Artifacts or Data That Is Not Measurable

At some point, someone within your organizational hierarchy or chain of command will want to know what you're doing with all that contextual data or with all the IOCs, signatures, definitions, rulesets, and artifacts that you're creating, distributing or using. Before you do anything, make sure you know how, or even whether, what you're doing can be measured and evaluated. If you receive a CTI report that has 30 pages of an executive summary at the front and 5 pages of indicators in the back, some of the first questions to ask are:

- How will I get those indicators into a digital format?
- What detection, defensive and protection resources should receive them? (They depend on your intelligence and priority intel requirements.)
- How do we measure the success, failure, effectiveness and status of these indicators?
- What is the shelf life of these indicators? It's OK if you don't know or can't estimate it. Make sure to loop back to them at a reasonable point so you can assign a time to live (TTL).

Creating Less Internal CTI Than You Consume from External Sources

The best type of threat intel is the threat intel that you generate based on your own organization's environment. As we discussed in Chapter 2: Knowing What's Normal, you've got to understand your own environment to effectively use actionable and relevant CTI.

Not Generating Attacker Intelligence

An organization or enterprise that is large or important enough to be worth an advanced persistent threat actor's time has a strategic need to know its attackers. Although it's best to generate your own attacker intelligence based on what is happening within your environment, this is one area where it pays to use strategic products from a professional intelligence provider.

Attacker intelligence refers to topics like these:

- Observe

- Learn
- Prioritize intel requirements related to a specific attacker
- Adapt and adjust while that attacker is attempting to get into your organization or is already in
- Defend and react
- Prevent and track
- Disrupt and deter

You may be under extreme pressure to stop the pain of an incident by blocking or quarantining an attacker immediately. However, there is a case to be made to observe, learn and assess what they are doing. There are ways to do this without directly taking an evasive action (like reimaging an endpoint) and losing the opportunity to learn. There are options for standing up honeynets and various deception or "canary" resources. You can also disrupt and deter—wrap up the threat actor in a virtual LAN of death or isolate them to an area of your network where you can watch them operate.

This is known as MADNB—Monitor and Do Not Block. You may need upper management to support such a plan.

Participating in CTI Data or Indicator Dumping

Dumping is the practice of continually creating non-relevant or non-actionable CTI reports or objects (IOCs, signatures, definitions, rules) and throwing them indiscriminately into your detection products and platforms. It is a common problem in all security operations execution and it is a gross dereliction of duty. Dumping leads to a bunch of false positives, with little to no information about why the objects are still deployed months or years after their effective detection life.

This happens a lot, especially when impractical, non-achievable or arbitrary values are picked for measurements. A US Army Lieutenant, new to the field of Information Security but fresh out of Information Assurance six-week training, once told me, "Mr. Brown, I need you to create 25 IDS signatures a day and tell all of the senior analysts that they need to do the same". That lieutenant was using an arbitrary number written on a statement of work, created years ago by a contracting officer, as a metric for measuring on performance. I asked that Lieutenant if it mattered whether they were "good signatures" or "bad signatures". The answer was, "It doesn't matter. We just need to show we are writing at least 25 signatures per day, per analyst". That is a classic example of indicator dumping or CTI object dumping.

Threat and Intel Analysts Who Aren't Well-Rounded

I won't say it's easy, because our industry doesn't have enough security professionals to go around, but it is not very hard to find experienced, knowledgeable and skilled info/cyber security analysts who have little or no experience as CTI analysts. There are threat and intel analysts experienced doing traditional intel along the lines of Human Intelligence (HUMIT), Signals Intelligence (SIGINT), Geographical Intelligence (GEOINT) and Technical Intelligence (TECHINT) who have no infosec analyst experience. It is extremely rare to find the optimal mix of both. It's OK if you're more experienced and skilled in one category than the other. However, if you have no experience in one category, you'd better come up to speed quickly.

If you have experience, background and skills as an analyst as well as in CTI, *ask for a raise.*

Fusing CTI Objects with Security Detection Resources

Once you create or obtain IOCs, signatures, definitions, artifacts, rules, and other objects, and you have the proper context and association with your intel or priority intel requirements, it's time to push them out and manage their lifecycle. This is one of the most important parts of your CTI efforts. The challenge is that there are very few vectors or resources to do this. FireEye provides APIs on the Endpoint Security (HX) platform, on the Central Management (CM) platform, and others. Those APIs can be leveraged to move objects around, integrate products and platforms with other security resources, and more. The FireEye Security Orchestration platform can be tremendously valuable for automation and orchestration.

Another option is to integrate a TIP—a Threat Intel Platform—into your security operations resources. Manually creating and keying in all the CTI objects you collect or create doesn't scale well enough to meet the needs of a mature, robust CTI program. A TIP provides a way of pulling together threat intel feeds, aggregating or collating them, maturing them from RAW format to curated or synthetic objects (depending on your security products), and distributing them to as many security resources as possible for automatic ingestion. This isn't something you can easily do on your own. There are various threat intel platforms. Some enterprise-level, global customers use www.threatconnect.com ,which specializes in ingesting multiple types of indicators and then connecting to multiple resources to distribute and manage them.

Before you decide how to centrally collect or manage your CTI objects, you need to decide how many formats or "standards" to use and support. (There is no standard format accepted by all resources, with the same terms, categories, definitions, and so on.)

Types of Indicators, Signatures, Definitions, and Artifacts

This section lists some popular formats for defining, creating, categorizing and constructing various types of CTI objects. It is not a definitive or complete list.

OpenIOC Format: OpenIOC provides a standard format and terms for describing the artifacts encountered during the course of an investigation. Reference: https://www.fireeye.com/blog/threat-research/2013/10/openioc-basics.html

CAPEC: The Common Attack Pattern Enumeration and Classification (CAPEC) effort provides a publicly available catalog of common attack patterns that helps users understand how adversaries exploit weaknesses in applications and other cyber-enabled capabilities. Terms for attack patterns include:

- HTTP Response Splitting (CAPEC-34)
- Session Fixation (CAPEC-61)
- Cross Site Request Forgery (CAPEC-62)
- SQL Injection (CAPEC-66)
- Cross-Site Scripting (CAPEC-63)
- Buffer Overflow (CAPEC-100)
- Clickjacking (CAPEC-103)
- Relative Path Traversal (CAPEC-139)
- XML Attribute Blowup (CAPEC-229)

Reference: https://capec.mitre.org/data/definitions/542.html

STIX: Structured Threat Information Expression (STIX) is a language and serialization format that enables organizations to share CTI with one another in a consistent and machine-readable manner, helping security communities better understand what computer-based attacks they are most likely to see and to anticipate and respond to those attacks faster and more effectively. STIX is designed to improve many different capabilities, such as collaborative threat analysis, automated threat exchange, automated detection and response, and more.
Reference: https://oasis-open.github.io/cti-documentation/
https://www.mitre.org/capabilities/cybersecurity/overview/cybersecurity-blog/stix-20-finish-line

TAXII: Trusted Automated Exchange of Intelligence Information (TAXII™) is an application-layer protocol used to exchange cyber threat intelligence (CTI) over HTTPS. TAXII enables organizations to share CTI by defining an API that aligns with common sharing models. TAXII is specifically designed to support the exchange of CTI represented in STIX.

Reference: https://oasis-open.github.io/cti-documentation/
https://www.mitre.org/publications/technical-papers/the-trusted-automated-exchange-of-indicator-information-taxii%E2%84%A2

CybOX: The Cyber Observable Expression (CybOX™) language provides a common structure for representing cyber observables across the operational areas of enterprise cyber security. CybOX improves the consistency, efficiency, and interoperability of deployed tools and processes, and it increases overall situational awareness by enabling detailed automatable sharing, mapping, detection, and analysis heuristics. CybOX has been integrated into STIX version 2.0.

MAEC: Malware Attributed Enumeration and Characterization (MAEC) is a language similar to STIX that is used to describe malware behavior from the very low technical level up to the more abstract, contextual levels of behaviors and capabilities.
Reference: https://makingsecuritymeasurable.mitre.org/docs/maec-intro-handout.pdf

Closing the Loop with Your Own Threat Intel

There are many points where you can close the loop to create your own CTI, thus generating your own indicators, attacker profiles, signatures, definitions, artifacts, and so on. You can also create pivot or injection points within security operating tasks and workflow where CTI can be applied. To do either, you must know your own processes and, optimally, have them documented. You also must have visibility into when these processes are happening. Neither is easy.

Here are two scenarios where you can either use CTI or create your own strategic reports or tactical CTI objects.

Penetration Tests and Red Teaming

Penetration testing and red teams often generate deliverables such as post-penetration test reports and red team exercise summaries. While these reports are very helpful at a management level and should be useful to your defensive and protection activities, it often isn't obvious how those reports or information can be turned into actionable indicators. Another challenge is getting those actionable indicators back into your environment for detection, scanning, sweeping, enterprise searching or real-time detection with IOCs.

For example, your pen test team has exploited a vulnerability that effectively disabled Windows 7 and Windows 8 user authentication control (UAC). To do this, they injected a process-altering DLL into three Windows files that are already categorized as "medium integrity" processes (documented at https://www.greyhathacker.net/?p=796).

For Windows 7, the process-altering DLL was successful with the following files:

- C:\Windows\Explorer.exe
- C:\Windows\System32\wuauclt.exe
- C:\Windows\System32\taskhost.exe

Once the three files above have been altered to allow UAC bypass, each process will have a different MD5. Those
MD5s should be provided to your CTI team. They can then be mapped to an intel or priority intel requirement (for example, PIR 4.3.x: Identify mechanisms for UAC bypass based on successful red team/pen testing exercise technique) and provided to your anomaly sensing and warning team or your content development team and used in scanning, sweeping or searching across your enterprise.

You may need to have a deconfliction component to determine whether the results returned were generated by the pen test exercise or by a threat actor.

Pivoting from an Alert

In this example, your CTI strategic team has received a report stating that five of your competitors in the retail industry have been compromised by a specific variant of GhostRAT. Based on the intrusions, the report contains several C2 (command and control) IPs.

- Your CTI strategic team passes those C2 IPs to the tactical team. Neither team has a threat intelligence platform or a security operations platform that includes threat intel management capabilities. They manually create synthetic or curated C2 IP indicators that can be uploaded to your SIEM for firewall and proxy analysis as well as for your endpoint detection and protection platform. Those indicators and rulesets are deployed.

- You run correlation rules against the firewall and proxy logs and deploy an IOC with the C2 IPs to your endpoint detection and protection platform. You discover five endpoints that either have engaged in session traffic to the malicious C2 IPs (discovered through ARP/networks stat cache details) or are currently engaged in session traffic (based on remote IP and port recon).

- After running a live response/scripted data acquisition on each endpoint, you determine which process identifiers, process names and files associated with the malicious process are involved. Now you have MD5s.

- You submit those malicious files to your dynamic analysis resource (such as the FireEye AX Series platform). You now have mutexes and a few registry keys you can use for detection.

- With the MD5s, mutexes and registry keys, you can now sweep your environment to look for other deployments of malware that are currently active or inactive. You discover 12 other endpoints compromised by the same malware under different file names, based on either mutex and registry hits on endpoints where the malware is inactive, or remote IP and port activity on endpoints where the malware is active.

This is an example of pivoting through alerts or pulling on the loose thread in the sweater, where you used a few known C2 IPs to discover 5 compromised endpoints initially and a further 12 based on your analytic workflow. The original "tipper" objects, the C2 IPs, were provided by your CTI strategic and tactical teams.

Convoy Briefings and Pre-Flight Crew Briefings

When you travel in a military convoy in areas like Iraq and Afghanistan, there is typically a threat and intelligence lead briefing before the convoy rolls out. Briefings provide non-classified knowledge about broad topics such as route information, risk levels, situational awareness, maybe a weather briefing, details about lead vehicles and trailing vehicles in the convey—anything that could affect safety. In commercial aviation, before anyone boards a commercial aircraft, the flight crew holds a pre-flight briefing that includes the captain, first officer and flight attendants. Passengers always receive a passenger briefing about basic safety, usually in multiple languages.

A CTI analyst or manager can do a similar team briefing before a security operations team starts its shift. I haven't yet encountered any organizations that do this (if your organization is doing this, please let me know). CTI pre-shift briefings don't have to be long or highly detailed, but they can include things like the following:

- The big incidents from yesterday and the plan to scan or sweep for indicators relating to them in the future

- Malware and threat actor details acquired from incidents at similar organizations, with an estimate of how vulnerable your organization is to the same malware or exploit

- Short recaps from your security operations admins or engineers about any detection and protection resources that are in a degraded state, undergoing maintenance or upgrades, or non-operational, with estimates of when they will return to full operation and availability

- Recommendations for threat hunting activities over the next 24–48 hours, based on threat and intel related to indicators of compromise, signatures, definitions, and artifacts created over the past 24–48 hours (I refer to this as a "similar/like/near" hunting mission)

- Your security operations team's progress relative to intelligence requirements and priority intelligence requirements.

- Lessons learned from the previous shift

This threat and intel briefing is a fantastic opportunity to collect feedback, observations and assessments from the ending shift to work into various strategies and tactics. The briefing doesn't have to be daily; it can be a "focused operation" activity that happens once a week.

Pain Points for Threat and Intel Teams

Most CTI teams believe that they should be doing everything possible to make their products, reports, assessments, observations or recommendations "deep and scary". This is also known as *alarmist syndrome* or *alarmist rhetoric*. This can happen to varying degrees. Your CTI team should not be known as the alarmists of your security operations organization. CTI ultimately is all about risk. Just because we can see that a set of C2 domains or IPs are registered to entities in China, Russia or Iran doesn't automatically mean they are involved in nation-state or intrusion/problem-set/APT activity. This leads me to the first pain point.

Incorrect Attribution

Management or leadership will often pressure a team for attribution. No one wants to hear, "We don't know who was responsible for this". It isn't uncommon to "stretch" for an answer when you feel this kind of pressure. That "stretch" might be based on a fraction of solid information and a fraction of guessing – what we sometimes call a swag, or a "scientific wild-ass guess". That "stretch" could also be random speculation. Just because you can associate malware with a C2 server hosted in a country that has engaged in nation-state sponsored hacking doesn't prove you've just been hit by an "APT". As we'll highlight in the next chapter, Advanced Persistent Threat is a style or technique, but it's often confused with specific groups for attribution. Furthermore, associating intel with a specific threat actor **does not exclude** other origins.

Consider Zeus, a frequently used malware package. Zeus was designed to steal financial information and was originally known as banking malware. Zeus has multiple functions, two of which are "man in the middle" and keylogging capabilities. Over the years, the source code for Zeus was released and turned into a framework that extends well beyond financial malware. There are variations such as GameOver.Zeus and InfoStealer/Zbot. It has been used as the base code for CryptoLocker ransomware. Customers and students I've taught have described experiences with Zeus and its variants that range from what was probably non-targeted, commodity malware showing no evidence of a higher-end attack all the way up to attacks tied to multiple advanced threat actors. Attribution to the source is difficult when source code and variants are widely available.

Subscription, Closed Source or "Private Label" Intel Is Better

Like anything else in life, intel has good sources, average sources and bad sources. Many groups pay massive amounts of money for subscription-based, private label or proprietary intelligence. Many government and military groups around the world use closed source or classified threat and intel feeds. While all of these are useful, using a private source doesn't guarantee that intel from your sources is measurable, actionable or relevant. Every source will say their cyber threat and intel finished products are wonderful. The decision about which is better doesn't rest with the vendor; it rests with you.

That's where most organizations fail – they bring in a lot of resources, reports, threat and intel product from subscription or closed source vendor platforms, but they never address whether the intel they receive is *measurable*. Before you decide on anything, if you can't come to grips with what needs to be measured along with a solid structure for gathering the telemetry and measuring it, it's all a guessing game.

This is very much easier to say (or write) than to execute. You may need the assistance of a third party or outside resource experienced with CTI measurement, collection or capture of data and telemetry, with the ability to evaluate and report on details like "return on investment" or "level of indicator actionability over a 30, 60 or 90-day horizon". Did your CTI provider give you a feed of 250 unique strings to search for in malware objects that would provide a high level of confidence in attribution? That's great! However, do you have a method of using them? If you do, how do you measure their effectiveness? Those are difficult questions and you cannot reasonably expect the answers from the vendor. As I often say, "It's not ours to provide, it's yours to measure".

Single-Source Observations, Assessments and Recommendations

Single-source intel could be intel that comes from only one threat and intel analyst on your team. Single-source could also mean hanging your hat on one source report or driving all your threat and intel based on one source's read on the topic. In CTI as in everything else, it's in your best interest to run everything through at least two or three other sources to raise the confidence level in your observations. This is often referred to as *analysis of competing hypotheses,* or ACH.

Richard J. Heuer Jr. authored a book that I highly recommend called *Psychology of Intelligence Analysis,* available freely on the US Central Intelligence Agency's public website at:

https://www.cia.gov/library/center-for-the-study-of-intelligence/csi-publications/books-and-monographs/psychology-of-intelligence-analysis

He defines ACH in the first line of Chapter 8: "A tool to aid judgement on important issues requiring careful weighting of alternative explanations or conclusions. It helps an analyst overcome, or at least minimize, some of the cognitive limitations that make prescient intelligence analysis so difficult to achieve".

Integrating Your CTI and Threat Hunting Teams

There are multiple advantages to integrating your CTI and threat hunting teams. The one I'd like to highlight is the advantage of integration when the volume of alerts or incidents appears to drop or level off. That can happen for various reasons. Sensor or detection capabilities can deteriorate or fail. You can lose visibility to an increase in HTTPS, SSL, and TLS and a decline in non-secure protocols. There may be a gap in detection capabilities between your Windows devices and your macOS and Linux devices.

Some indicators simply are too tight or restrictive to work more than once—for example, automatically created indicators that were sourced from a sandbox or dynamic analysis product. Computers write indicators as a computer would—they are very static in nature. They won't help when the object that was dynamically analyzed is a polymorphic piece of malware. I encourage all my students to double-check anything that is automatically created, when possible, and to run the object on which the indicator is based with a dynamic analysis device that allows the submitter to be in control of the submission configuration. If you run an object three or four times and notice that it behaves differently each time (different dropper/payload names, different deployment directories, varying registry key names created in locations like \runonce or \autorun in a Microsoft operating system), you're dealing with a polymorphic piece of malware. That means the automatic signature or indicator most likely will not work more than once.

Your threat and intel team can be leveraged when alert volume drops or stops. Give them a block of indicators, definitions, signatures, artifacts and have them run CTI analyst work against them. Various threat and intel reports may provide enhanced context and background about where those conditions have been seen in the past or how they might be relevant in different scenarios. Your

CTI team can review whether signatures, indicators, definitions, artifacts, and so on match with current intel or priority intel requirements. They can also provide objects to your threat hunting team for what I like to call a "similar/like/near" hunt mission.

When a set of signatures, indicators, definitions, and artifacts that produced a large volume of alerts in the past now seems to have leveled off, your threat hunting team can bounce them against a set of logs or packets, maybe even memory or hard drive images. They can hunt for patterns or indications of similar, like or near conditions and occurrences. A signature or indicator doesn't have to match a threat actor's malware exactly in order to be effective. As in the game shuffleboard or the military use of grenades, they don't have to be exact to be effective. It's enough just to be "in the zone."

Should your hunt team find something of interest, it's time to loop in the creators of custom detection content. The content would need to be a regular expression or YARA variable based or integrated into a detection capability that can match pattern or behavioral characteristics. That might also mean writing multi-stage or chained rule conditions in a SIEM or data analytics platform or using a product or platform that can create "analytics packs".

Retroactive Analysis as a CTI Team's Task

Many security resources are very much present-oriented. They constantly bounce indicators, signatures, definitions, rulesets, artifacts against packets in flow on the network or against data cached on the endpoint that is limited to a brief window in time. Even SIEMS and big data analytics platforms have limits on how they engage with correlation rules or rulesets. They may evaluate them against a stream of data or against a set of data captured from device logs, but after that, the data is moved to archives or retention stores. When you have a new analytic technique, a new indicator, an updated blacklist, or a revised active list of known malicious C2 IPs, the new item typically is not bounced against retroactive or historical data. That is a technique that some hunting teams employ; it can also be a used by your CTI team.

This technique is effective because it leverages the law of averages in your favor and against a threat actor engaged in evasive tactics. Attackers frequently like to jump domains and IP addresses, move across multiple URLS, or jump original autonomous system numbers that ISPs use for border gateway routing. If you bounce new indicators against older data, it's only a matter of time until you match activity. A match with this technique often indicates that a threat actor has been in your environment. It also may be a solid indication that your threat actor is more advanced because of how long they've been able to lie undetected in the network.

Chapter 12: Advanced/Nation-State Threat Actors

No book on security operations execution or security operations teams would be complete without a chapter on advanced and nation-state actors, otherwise known as Advanced Persistent Threat (APT) actors. A wide body of knowledge has been amassed over the years about these groups of intruders. I've even heard some say that these should not be considered "groups" and instead should be considered "styles" since attribution can be so difficult.

A common (though unattributed) definition in the information security industry is this: "APTs deceive you in their silent presence on your networks, degrade your ability to secure your intellectual property (or at minimum degrade your 'perceived' level of security), destroy your already diminishing confidence in COTS security products to prevent or detect them, and directly influence the way you sleep at night."

Two books on the subject that I recommend are:

- *Advanced Persistent Threat: Understanding the Danger and How to Protect Your Organization* by Dr. Eric Cole of SANS. Although the book is six years old, it is still a valuable reference and an enjoyable read.
- *Reverse Deception: Organized Cyber Threat Counter-Exploitation* by Sean Bodmer and Dr. Max Kilger. This book has a very solid set of criteria for targeting groups.

FireEye also provides a wide range of products, dossiers, reports, and digital indicators that are subscription-based or closed source. The gateway to these resources is the FireEye iSight Intelligence Portal (FIIP).

This chapter covers broad incident response and handling topics that security operations teams should think about when they find themselves wrapped up with an advanced threat actor incident, set of incidents, intrusion or set of intrusions. This isn't a typical APT chapter—I focus on strategy once you know that you're dealing with an APT intrusion.

The Terminology Problem

As in other aspects of information security, different vendors and different security communities use different terminology for these groups. While many refer to these groups as APTs, a segment of the information security population objects to that term because many advanced groups begin with simple initial compromise techniques such as social engineering and waterholes. Other common terms are:

- ATA: Advanced Threat Actor
- I/P-Set: Intrusion/Problem-Set (widely used by the US government)
- TCOGs: Targeting Cyber Operations Group
- FO: Focused Operators
- NaStaSTA: Nation-State Sponsored Threat Adversary
- TIO: Targeted Information Operations
- TFO: Tailored Focused Operations

Even a single threat actor can have various names from different vendors or resources. The following terms are all names for the same group:

- APT1—The name Mandiant assigned to the threat group believed to be associated with China's military unit 61398, documented in the APT1 report from February 2013.
- STAR—An older name for the same group used by companies in the US defense industry.
- The Comment Crew—The unofficial IS community name for the same group. This group is notorious for sprinkling command and control (C2) signals deep in compromised web servers as HTML comments. The comments are never rendered in browsers and can only be found by examining HTML code.
- Y29 Crew—Another unofficial name, used because all of the group's C2 signaling starts with Y29 (the Base64 encoded representation for the letters *co*).
- Comment Panda—A name assigned by CrowdStrike.
- TG-8223—A name assigned by Dell SecureWorks.
- BrownFox—A name assigned by iSight Threat Intelligence before iSight was acquired by FireEye.
- Group3—A name assigned by Cisco.
- US CYBERCOM and NSA—Classified military designators.

FireEye avoids creative names in its publicly available blogs, webcasts and other technical material. Instead, we use the following names, with a number assigned to designate a particular group:
- APTx—Advanced persistent threat group, such as APT1 or APT28
- FINx—Financially oriented advanced threat actor group, such as FIN1 or FIN5
- INDx—Industry-oriented advanced threat actor group, such as IND2 or IND4
  UNKx—Unknowngroup, such as UNK1 or UNK2

In the military and in defense contracting, many intrusion/problem-set groups are categorized by their ability to engage in one or more of the following activities:

- CNO—Computer Network Operations
- CNE—Computer Network Exploitation
- CAN—Computer Network Attack

The Skepticism Problem

The retired general and former NSA Chief Keith Alexander has said that the costs associated with responding to computer hacking represents "the greatest transfer of wealth in history". Unfortunately, there are still some in the IT community who believe APTs don't exist. They refer to APTs as "Advanced Persistent Marketing" and consider them to be a scare tactic used by vendors to sell products. While these skeptics and "pundits" are becoming rarer, their attitude disturbs those of us who have direct experience with these threat actors. When you have documented session commands that were run over hours or days, and you can match that "playbook" up with other customers in the same business segment who have experienced the same intrusions, it's no coincidence.

The consequences of ignoring APTs can be serious or even fatal to an organization. Here are two cautionary examples.

Titan Rain

Titan Rain was a cyber espionage ring based in China. In 2005, Shawn Carpenter strongly suspected that his employer, Sandia National Labs, was deeply infiltrated by this group. Instead of being supported, enabled, and rewarded for his efforts, he was fired and stripped of his Department of Energy Q clearance. Shawn spent months of his own time tracking the Titan Rain group and communicating his findings to the FBI. He was eventually proved right; Titan Rain had already compromised at least one major military base. He also won a defamation and wrongful termination lawsuit against Sandia National Labs. He has invested the millions from the lawsuit in multiple cyber security, threat and intelligence companies. To this day, his work endures.

Nortel

About 10 years after Titan Rain, Nortel Networks Corporation outsourced much of its manufacturing to the Chinese company Huawei. Soon the project engineering was also being done by Huawei. It is believed that the Chinese built "back doors" into the products and eventually used them to thoroughly infiltrate Nortel's corporate system. Brian Shields, one of the technical editors of this book, was on the front lines of what happened at Nortel and a first-hand witness to what happens when an advanced threat group is targeting your company. Nortel was once the dominant player in business telephony; the company declared bankruptcy in 2009 and all its business units were sold off in 2011.

The Attribution Problem

Not very long ago, if you detected past or current persistent network connections to or from certain academic or university organizations in foreign countries, you could conclude they were probably APT-related. In Operation Aurora, the intrusion into Google in 2010 by the Chinese Elderwood Group and Unit 61398, multiple connections were associated with process identifiers assigned to custom malware that was used in communications to and from Shaghai Jiao Tong University and Lanxiang Vocational School. Both of those educational institutions have also been engaged in communication sessions involved with malware detected during other intrusions at different companies, and the victim targets have been grouped together by similar business functions. (Both institutions denied those allegations, but packet captures don't lie.) Today the correlation with certain universities needs to be considered along with a matrix of other factors, but it can still be strongly weighted in an evaluation.

On the other hand, there are times when attribution is practically impossible. Some domestically located sites have been used in C2 APT activity without their owners' knowledge. When law enforcement showed up to investigate, the impacted organization were just as surprised as anyone. Analysis and endpoint and network forensics discovered that the "evil" C2 server was another victim being used as an intermediary or cat's paw by the real attacker. The tiered or staged C2 hierarchy looked like Figure 60:

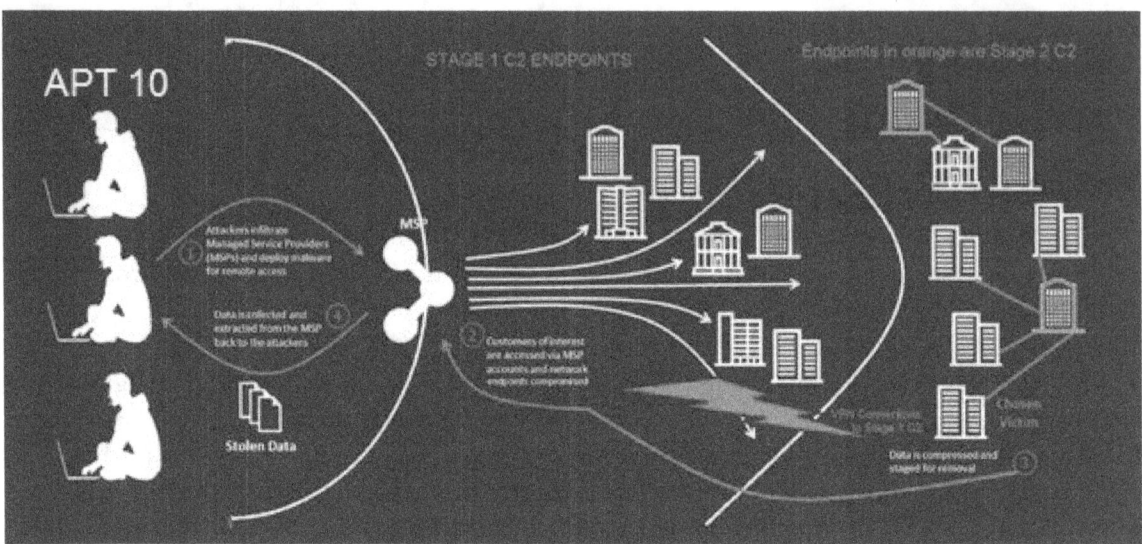

Figure 60: Staged C2 hierarchy

The systems in stage 2 (on the right) are being used as C2 servers. They are connected through VPNs to various universities and academic institutions (center), which can be used as stage 1 C2 servers controlled by the real threat group. Those institutions may not know they're victims, let alone attackers. They were compromised through a common Managed Service Provider (MSP) used by multiple academic and university institutions.

This is an example where attribution can take an unexpected turn and become nearly impossible. It also shows why "attacking back" at the perceived attacker is generally a bad idea—you might unwittingly target the wrong organization.

Techniques of Advanced Threat Actor Groups

The common techniques used by Advanced Threat Actor Groups are well known and thoroughly described elsewhere. I want to touch on a few in this section.

Initial Compromise Using Basic Methods

Many APT groups start with the simplest methods of attack. This is one reason that a single group may have so many names. (It's also the reason that some security professionals don't like to use the word "Advanced" in the name.) Often they use initial compromise techniques like spear phishing or social engineering to get users to access malicious websites. Or they use waterholes, where exploits tailored for a targeted organization are launched from a website frequented only by certain populations of users, many of whom are connected to the organization. There typically isn't a valid reason to use the advanced intrusion methods when the known or more simple methods still work. A threat actor group avoids burning an advanced resource for an initial compromise because once it's detected, a defense can be mounted quickly and the resource becomes unusable.

Multihoming to Droppers

Have you ever marveled at how multimedia providers like NetFlix and YouTube are able to stream videos and audio smoothly even to endpoints under serious bandwidth constraints? One resource providers use for this is known as *adaptive transmission routing protocols*—routing protocols that dynamically adapt to various network conditions. These protocols and transmission methods were originally developed to transport high levels of high-bandwidth data to low-bandwidth targets. Some of the more innovative advanced threat actors use the same resources for their own operational resiliency. It's common knowledge that a single endpoint can reach out to multiple C2 servers. It's less well known that advanced threat actors also use multihomed or distribution servers to push C2 signals *in reverse*. Some of them might even be riding the backs of multimedia providers to get their C2 established. This advanced technique is not used by "script kiddies" or commodity malware pushers. It is in the province of massive cybercrime campaigns or APT/focused operations incidents and compromises.

Some inline network security devices have a hard enough time dealing with packets, extracting objects and re-constructing sessions at the packet level. Dealing with multihomed streaming sessions that come from hundreds or thousands of streams is a nightmare of content and packet disassembly, evaluation and reassembly. Some detection and defensive products flat out fail under those conditions because their packet pre-processors and parsers were never designed to evaluate multimedia session streams that have been hijacked.

Evading Detection by Avoiding Detection Infrastructure

Some advanced threat actors understand that one of the best ways to evade detection is to avoid detection grids and sensors altogether ("living off the land"). Techniques for this include the following:

- Not using malware
- Creating tools on the fly in memory
- Hollowing out processes or riding in processes that are whitelisted or trusted
- Spreading tool creation over multiple streaming sessions that most detection pre-processors won't keep their "buckets" open long enough to re-construct
- Running malware from trusted black-box appliances that are exempt from security policy or are not patched or scanned frequently

These techniques make both static detection and dynamic analysis extremely difficult because malicious activity appears to be benign and uses the same resources used by a systems, endpoint or network administrator.

Controlled Response Versus "Stop It All Now!"

Stay calm and try NOT to freak out—that's what they are hoping you'll do.

Large-scale mistakes can easily happen when pressure is applied. I've seen experienced, smart incident responders do things they normally wouldn't under the stress of a massive APT intrusion. For instance, earlier we discussed the risks of submitting objects to external resources. Your security operations team may have the best intentions and policies in place, with a firm resolve to fully review everything before submission externally in order to remove credentials, hostnames, certificates, and so on. During an APT incident, all of those good intentions may fly out the window. As the boxer Mike Tyson said in July 2015, when he was asked how worried he was about Evander Holyfield and his fight plan, "Everyone has a plan until they get punched in the mouth".

The "fight or flight" response is natural—when you discover an attack, you want to leap to defend yourself. But remember—they expect you to do that. Nation-state sponsored threat actors have spent a lot of time, money and resources to target and reconnoiter your organization, and they are likely to have multiple plans for dealing with evasive remediation or extraction. Like any organization, they plan for redundancy, resiliency, recoverability, failover, and so on.

Suppose a threat actor has compromised a fleet of endpoints. If two or three endpoints are lost, they may consider that routine attrition as endpoints are removed for maintenance, or shut down during someone's vacation. Loss of a block of endpoints may be interpreted as an evasive action signaling that they have been detected. Advanced threat actors who they think they're going to lose it all may jump to the *opposite* end of the infected fleet so they can implant more malware or laterally jump to other systems.

The following sections provide important things to consider while you're staying calm—*before* you jump into drastic action. The best way to win a race with an adversary is not to let the adversary realize that you're in the race!

Your Established Modes of Communication Will Be Targeted First

An advanced threat actor will want to say tuned in to what is happening and two of the first resources they will attempt to compromise are the communication resources used by your security operations teams:

- Email
- Knowledge Management sites (SharePoint, Jive, Wikis)
- Portals for documents, diagrams, network layouts, application architecture, and so on
- Chat and instant messaging apps (ICQ, WhatsApp, Microsoft Teams)
- IT service management and ticketing applications (Remedy, ServiceNow, HP Service Desk)

Email and service management or ticketing applications are frequently targeted for compromise first.

One organization where I've taught had previously been breached so deeply by an APT actor that everything they sent through email was being read by the threat actor. When they realized this, they had to regroup and consider how to proceed. Their decision was to give everyone in InfoSec 2-way radios for communication instead of email. When I showed up, everyone still had those radios attached to their belts or backpacks. Being a ham radio operator, I smiled and asked, "What happens when the threat actor that you think is overseas stations a person in your parking lot with the same type of radio, tuned to the same frequency, able to covertly monitor or record your every move?" They didn't appreciate my cynicism, but the reality is, there's always a counter to any defense. Albert Gonzalez, leader of the cyber crime groups Shadowcrew and Operation Get Rich or Die Tryin', used exactly this technique to compromise many of his targets. He sat in a car or a van in the parking lots of his victims and passively scooped up all the WiFi signals he could until he had enough to start his hacking work.

The reality is that most organizations will not shut down a majority of the infrastructure they need for day-to-day business. You need a plan for *operational resiliency.*

Your Centrally Integrated Resources for Authentication and Authorization Will Be Used Against You

If your organization relies on centrally integrated authentication and authorization resources, attackers will use them against you. This includes:

- Active Directory
- LDAP
- TACACS+
- AAA (Authentication, Authorization and Accounting) servers

Be aware that the risk profile of centrally managed accounts dramatically increases during an APT incident. Attackers compromise those central accounts to get administrative or root credentials that they can use to access network resources throughout your enterprise. The probability of this happening is not low. In my experience, an attacker needs to compromise only 3-5 systems on average before they find cached credentials they need for domain-level privilege escalation. At that point, an attacker typically runs into an endpoint touched remotely by someone from the helpdesk or application support. The credentials used by your admins—maybe when they perform a vulnerability scan or a penetration test—are cached, and sometimes those caches persist in memory for weeks or month (I hope your patching and updating process requires endpoint reboots more frequently than that). On Microsoft operating systems, all a threat actor needs to do is to run wce.exe (Windows credential editor) to capture those cached credentials, move the output of wce.exe off the endpoint, and work on breaking into local admin or even domain or enterprise admin privileges—and it's game over.

Many organizations have policies that require all their IT and IS resources to be centrally managed. Audit and regulatory requirements often control whether resources can be managed by local accounts or centrally managed accounts. In every class I teach about deployment, support or administration, I cover the advantages and disadvantages of creating local accounts or integrating with LDAP or Active Directory. Instructors and consultants can train and advise you and even provide recommendations based on our experience and best practices. However, the decision is your call.

Deploying Security Resources After an APT Intrusion Is Too Late

Fortunately, most customers I've taught put their tooling and detection resources on endpoints as soon as they get approval. However, a few organizations that support a "culture of trust" do not push security resources to endpoints proactively, fearing a perception that the company employees are being spied upon or monitored. Instead, they reactively deploy agents or tooling to systems and attempt to put monitoring resources in place only after they know they're compromised. I hate to say this, but if you're working for a company like that, your biggest problem isn't the advanced threat actor—it's your company management. They are putting their concerns about perception ahead of their responsibility to protect IT resources, which means having the security tools and resources ready when they're needed.

I've even run into this in the military. Once when I was defense contracting, I knew with high confidence that an intrusion-problem set threat actor was running its C2 through various Skype chat channels. Because Skype logs everything, I wanted to acquire Skype logs and use their log viewing application (skypeviewer.exe) to parse malware C2 commands. However, I was told that that was an invasion of privacy. This on a US military network, when everyone who logs in at the beginning of a shift is explicitly told *not to expect privacy* and that their communications can be monitored or reviewed for operational and security concerns.

All security teams should bring this up with their organization or company before you're in the middle of an APT campaign. Don't be deterred by resistance from managers who say, "That can't happen here".

Your Endpoint Logs May Be More Relevant Than Your Domain Controller Logs

Having worked for multiple security vendors and spent 18.5 years delivering training and consulting, I've often told (and heard from) customers, "Just forward us the logs from your domain controllers." It would be a huge challenge to capture, process and store event logs from 50,000 endpoints. Sending the logs from a few hundred or even a few thousand domain controllers is a better compromise.

Guess who else hears that? Advanced threat actors. That advice has been around for decades. If an attacker knows that the target's security vendor recommends collecting domain controller logs, that attacker will do everything to *stay out of the domain controller logs* when they authenticate or log in. You can either authenticate and log in to a server/domain controller, or you can authenticate and log in locally.

Understandably, a global enterprise organization with anywhere from 50,000 to 400,000 or more endpoints can't realistically manage the collection, processing, storage and retention of so many endpoint logs. However, keep in mind that it often pays to look where you *don't* expect trouble. This extends to anything else you trust or add to a whitelist. I've seen malware hidden in hard drives integrated with printers and digital senders that exhibit abnormal network traffic to and from their network ports. Anything that has a hard drive and a network interface is a candidate for exploitation or malicious use—the more remote, obscure or unknown, the better.

APT Operators Monitor Their Own Infrastructure

Professional, structured APT threat actor groups care about the time and money invested in their work, just like you. Some don't even refer to their infrastructure as malicious droppers and C2 servers. They consider their droppers to be agents and their C2 servers to be collectors or connectors that integrate with their management servers. What we, as defenders, typically refer to as C2 signaling, they think of as beaconing or status signaling. They consider their malicious infrastructure communication to be every bit as legitimate as an application monitoring platform or a directory service product that was designed for IT infrastructure. Figure 61 shows a typical bot controller attackers use to monitor their own infrastructure.

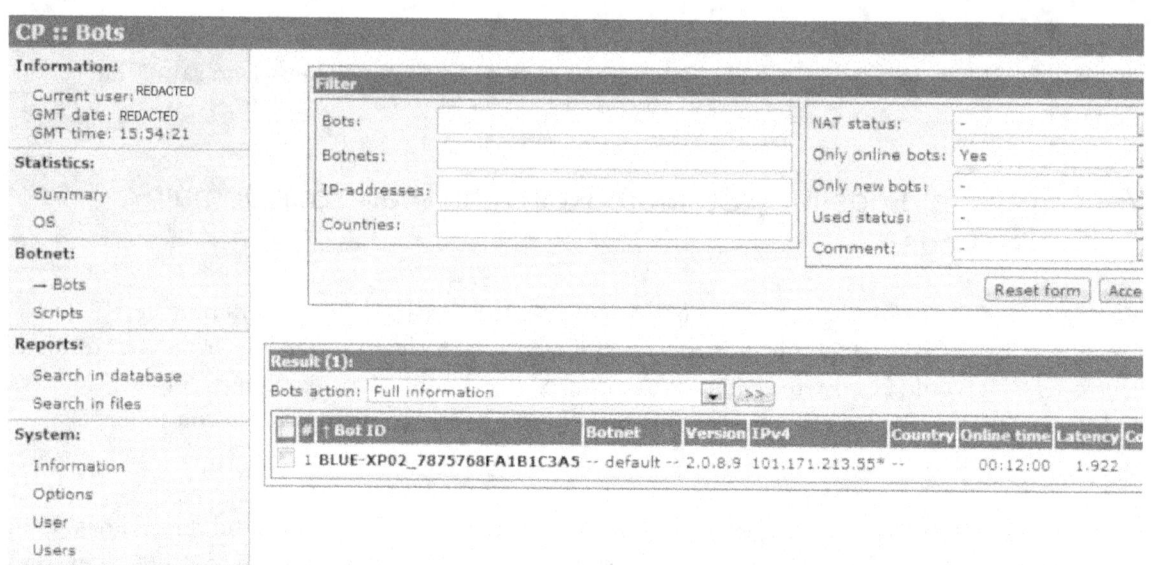

Figure 61: Bot controller

The Results section displays the Bot ID BLUE-XP02_7875768FA1B1C3A5. The string BLUE-XP02 contains the bot's hostname ("Blue") and its version of Windows ("XP02" for Windows XP service pack 2). The next string of characters is most likely the bot's globally unique identifier (GUID).

Information can be transmitted by various mechanisms—through a user agent string, or through a C2 channel that's encrypted from payload to a C2 server. I've seen malware that communicated over SNMP using their own Management Information Base (MIB) files with a malicious SNMP receiver deployed by the intruder. The internal SNMP receiver aggregated telemetry from tens of thousands of internal malware deployments and then synchronized everything through SSL in bulk sessions that rolled every 6 hours to external C2 servers. (If you use correlation rules with default aggregation settings like 1 event per hour, they would never fire for processes rolling once every 6 hours.) This type of staged architecture for C2 is typical of larger infrastructure malware deployed throughout a victim's enterprise network.

ATP groups and nation-state-sponsored threat actors react to the loss, damage, destruction or disruption of their previous work the same way we do. They plan for redundancy, resiliency, recoverability, fail over, and so on. They won't give up easily. If your response actions are not tailored for specific types of adversaries, they could be the equivalent of poking a hornet's nest with a fork.

Security Data Visualization for APT Intrusions

The tooling or resources you need for APT/intrusion-problem set threat actors needs to be able to rise to the occasion. It's tempting to have a one-size-fits-all security operations incident response/handling plan. However, different plans and responses are required for various types of threat actors. An incident response/handling plan that is great for commodity or hacktivism-related intrusions will probably not work well with an APT.

This is where I wish security data visualization were more advanced. Heat maps that show where new processes were being rapidly spawned could be a good indicator that something is moving quickly through your network. (Context would be needed because "spraying patches" across the enterprise can quickly create new processes, files or objects. Figure 62 shows an example (hostnames have been obfuscated).

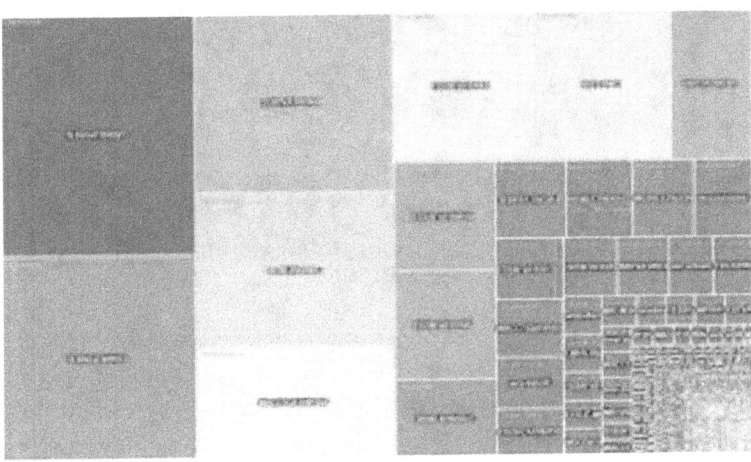

Figure 62: Heat map

You don't need to read the data tags to see that something massive is happening in the clusters on the lower right. When time is of essence, the right type of security data visualization will outperform alerts, events, and analysis.

Figure 63 shows Starlight, a product that was originally open source when it was created over 10 years ago by Pacific Northwest National Laboratory (PNNL). (Starlight was changed to closed source/commercial and then was returned to PNNL, and its current status is unclear.)

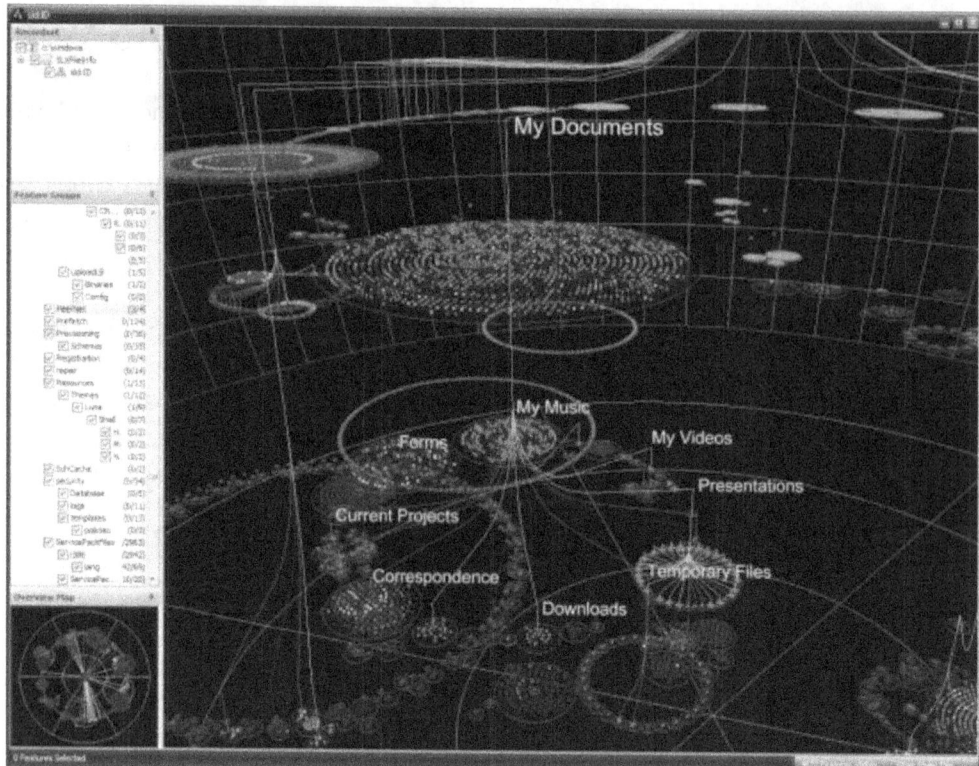

Figure 63: Starlight

Notice the density around My Documents and My Music. That information might not mean much during a lower-priority, non-targeted commodity or smash and grab incident. In an APT intrusion, however, it can be coupled with correlation—for example, it could display clusters of files across multiple systems that were accessed by WINRAR.EXE, detected through PreFetch "accessed files". Most security operations teams would want to know about this immediately, and it might take hours to get started manually analyzing PreFetch "accessed files" following an endpoint alert.

Chapter 13: Top Security Operations Themes

If you've made it this far in the book, congratulations. This chapter summarizes the top security operations themes of this book. A "top 10" list that had a strong impact on me in 2004, when I dedicated my career to information security and training, was Microsoft's Security list of "Ten Immutable Laws of Security". For example, Law #3 is "If a bad guy has unrestricted physical access to your computer, it's not your computer anymore". Originally published on the Microsoft TechNet blog, the ten laws can still be found here:

https://blogs.technet.microsoft.com/steve_lamb/2005/01/04/how-to-think-like-a-hacker-scott-culps-10-immutable-laws-of-security/

These top 10 laws of security are just as important to remember as the C-I-A triad of confidentiality, integrity and availability and the three key principles of authentication—what you have (such as a random-number-generating token), what you are (biometrics) and what you know (answers to security questions). For information security and information technology, knowing these is just as important as knowing the seven layers of the OSI model.

You probably learned the OSI layers using a mnemonic, such as "All People Seem To Need Data Processing" (top to bottom) or "People Definitely Need To See Paula Abdul" (bottom to top). If you've ever heard a teacher or instructor use a corny, cheesy, terrible joke in a lesson, we do those kinds of things for a reason. While you may not remember everything that was said in eight hours or five days of training, most people remember the times they were laughing. The lame jokes and crazy analogies help fix concepts and details in your mind. I hope the "laws" in this chapter help you remember they key themes of security information operations. I would love to hear from you about "top 10s" or key associations you've used in the past to remember critical information security topics.

#1 – The Devil Is in the Details

The ability to maintain focus and spot the details, no matter how minor they seem, is essential for anyone on a security operations team. For example, spotting the difference between ADMIN and ADM1N or looking at the details of TCP or IP headers is critical. Even knowing how commands like *tracert* execute under different operating systems can make the difference. A good example of subtle anomalies in HTTP headers—and the difficulty of spotting them—is presented in Chris Sander's blog on the topic of inattentional blindness (https://chrissanders.org/2015/08/inattentional-blindness/). This is one reason that security operations teams require a quiet working environment, away from traffic and background noise.

#2 – Things Are Not What They Appear to Be

In information security, as in illusions, magic, and professional wrestling, not everything is what it appears to be. Threat actors will do everything possible to avoid or evade detection, to appear normal, to make it difficult to distinguish malicious from benign behavior. You must look from multiple angles and take multiple snapshots, just as you need at least three detection points to identify the source of a radio or cell signal (triangulation).

To understand how polymorphic malware behaves, you need to run it multiple times and observe it dynamically. Three submissions or detonations might not be enough, depending on how polymorphic it is. This is one reason that static signatures fail on a wide scale. During incident response and handling, it's essential to take multiple acquisitions of network details or run multiple iterations of *netstat -anob* commands to analyze what has happened over time.

One technique is to start with the endpoints that are known or likely to be a point of intrusion or compromise. From there, do similar analysis on the systems that have the most network sessions with the compromised system, and so on. (If there are no ongoing network connectivity or sessions, NetFlow or router/switch logs may show past activity.)

While you may not find anything out of the ordinary, you never know unless you look.

Like any good analyst or hunter, don't stop if you don't find anything suspicious or potentially anomalous *currently* going on when you gather information about the top few systems that your compromised endpoint has traces of communications with (there may be no ongoing network connectivity or sessions but NetFlow or router/switch logs may show past activity). If there have been past sessions or traces of network traffic, it's still worth a look.

Dr. Edmond Locard stated the Locard Exchange Principle of forensic science: every contact leaves a trace. "Wherever (the criminal or in our case, the adversary) steps, whatever he touches, whatever he leaves, even unconsciously, will serve as a silent witness against him. Not only his fingerprints or his footprints, but his hair, the fibers from his cloths, the glass he breaks, the tool mark he leaves, the paint he scratches." One of our duties during incidents and intrusions is to track down the digital equivalents of fingerprints, footprints, and fibers.

#3 – Show Me the Data

Observations, assessments, summaries and theoretical ideas that flow throughout your information technology and security teams are great, but they must be backed up by solid data:

- Logs
- Packets
- Artifacts extracted from memory
- Objects carved out of full disk images
- Validation of IOCs (not the IOCs themselves, but data that supports them)

Every decision that is made within your security operations team should be data-driven. Use measurement data and telemetry to back up your hunches. Then validate them with data from a second and even a third source. Remember that details can change over time. Trust, but verify.

#4 – Ask Questions First and Shoot Later

When your endpoints show anomalies or fail en masse due to CryptoLocker Ransomware, you may feel a powerful urge to reimage and start fresh. In virtualized and cloud environments, WBR (wipe, baseline, redeploy) will immediately stop the pain. However, it also wipes out artifacts and evidence, which closes the door on many questions that your security team will have about the adversary's techniques. You also lose virtually all endpoint vectors for conducting any counterintelligence.

Reimaging may also throw your asset management or agent-based products into an unusual state. Every endpoint typically has an agent identification string, as well as SSL elements like public keys, certificates and private keys that can cause problems if they are re-issued too many times for the same endpoint.

There is a broad debate over whether to re-baseline or to attempt mitigation, cleanup and remediation. Your organization needs to weigh the pros and cons of each. You don't need to use the same response for everything. There are times when it's best to use quarantining, isolation, and containment and then work through post-intrusion steps. There may be other times when you've got commodity malware on endpoints and can't justify anything except re-imaging.

#5 – It's Not Ours to Prove; It's Yours to Measure

Information security vendors can provide all types of speeds and feeds, scalability numbers, details on how we think a certain product, platform or model number will perform under various conditions. We can tell you what our design requirements were and what our products platforms can and can't do. However, the only numbers that really count are the measurements and telemetry produced when the product runs in *your* environment.

FireEye software provides numerous commands and logs that you can leverage for performance measurement, trending, and telemetry extraction. Our technical publications, customer support and training organizations provides extensive documentation and troubleshooting courses. Use them to find out when platforms will go into bypass mode, when they start dropping packets, and how they behave during saturation or congestion. Your security operations team will often have tasks or missions to measure how your products and platforms are performing, reactively (and hopefully proactively) respond to small issues before they become big issues, monitor the storage utilized and available free space on various storage arrays, monitor-document and trend network interface stats, and so on. Those types of data are not ours to prove; they are *yours to measure.*

If you're not sure what data to collect and what to measure, one of the best books I've read on the subject is *A Data-Driven Computer Security Defense: THE Computer Security Defense You Should Be Using* by Roger A. Grimes. I highly recommend using that book as a resource to help shape your data-driven defense, detection and protection operations.

#6 – Without Context, They're Just Random Points of Data

All the data in the world is meaningless without the right context. Your security products generate all kinds of alerts, alarms, and events. You need context to help you distinguish what's anomalous from what's normal in your environment. Big data analytics and machine learning are moving our industry in the right direction. Advances in automation and orchestration help us with correlation.

#7 – Everyone Has a Plan Until They're Punched in the Mouth

The best plans, processes and procedures can vaporize when you find out that 15,000 of your production office endpoints were just hit with a master boot record wiper. How will your team react? Are you sure they will stay calm under pressure? One way to measure your team's reaction to a punch in the mouth is to discreetly plan for an exercise, like those run on battle cruisers and aircraft carriers. Exercises can be anything from table-top exercises to major missions. Although you may feel you too busy to spend time and resources on exercises, even one or two smaller exercises can be invaluable. For example, you can obtain malware that has been known to slip past other organizations, inject it into your environment (carefully—we often defang or sterilize malware first) and tell your team you were just visited by a DNS provider that says they've detected evil from endpoints on your network.

You may need the assistance of an outside organization to set up and provide for simulated attacks and intrusions. FireEye offers ThreatSpace cyber range training.

#8 – A Picture Is Worth a Thousand Log Lines

Security data visualization used with thought, planning and in the right circumstances can be dramatic and extremely time saving. I'm not talking about pie charts, bar charts, and other eye candy that impresses VIPs, but rich, dynamically updating visualizations that are relevant and actionable for your organization, such as IDS or IPS alert heat maps and correlation-driven density renderings. FireEye offers high-level threat maps and process diagramming in its OS Change Detail reports that you will find in Network, Email and File Security platforms. SNMP MIBS can be monitored and viewed through HP OpenView, Computer Associates Unicenter, SolarWinds and many other SNMP trap receivers.

I recently was teaching at a customer that worked on academic and lab research. I asked their threat hunting team if they really used the big 70-inch monitor displaying a bunch of red, green and yellow icons. Three members jumped up and showed me how they used it every day—swiping, double tapping, and drilling into some very meaningful and actionable detection and analytic programs. If a majority of your security operations team says, "Oh, we never pay any attention to that screen", it's time to reconsider your visualization.

#9 – If You're Not Doing Vulnerability Scans and Realistic Penetration Tests, Someone Else Is

… and that person doesn't work for you.

Detecting traffic and activity that reflect objects exploiting or being exploited, scanning for vulnerabilities and applying patches, may not be exciting. I've done my share of "spraying scans and throwing patches". However, it's *vital* to keep this up, monthly, weekly, even daily. Because your adversary is constantly scanning for weakness.

The same goes for *realistic* internal penetration or red team tests. Tests that are locked in to a narrow scope are not realistic or useful. Tests need to be no holds barred with wide scope (which is rare). Your pen testers and red teamers are the closest thing you'll have to an internal APT. Unfortunately, pen testers and red teams often are told to exclude important systems for fear of disrupting operations. Many options, such as social engineering, are taken off the table by the customer or requestor.

The hackers, threat actors and malicious intruders out there aren't so limited. As their skill, proficiency and effort increase, they will find a way in sooner or later if they have enough time, resources and patience.

Afterword

Well, as they say in Hollywood, that's a wrap. I hope you enjoyed this book. It has been quite a journey for me, my book editor and technical editors, and those who contributed feedback and recommendations.

I welcome feedback, constructive, negative or positive. Please send it to me by way of press@fireeye.com

If you enjoyed this book or if even one part of it resonated with you, please—tell someone. The only advertising that works well for these types of books is word of mouth. If this book was meaningful to you, I hope you'll recommend this book to your peers, colleagues or anyone who has an interest in information security.

Thank you, keep fighting the good fight, find evil, live long and prosper!

Chris "BigBiz" Brown
Formerly Sr. Technical Instructor
FireEye Products & Platforms – Deployment, Training & Readiness
FireEye Customer Success

www.ingramcontent.com/pod-product-compliance
Lightning Source LLC
Chambersburg PA
CBHW082034190526
45165CB00020B/2504